Parental Involvement in Primary Schools

R. Cyster
P. S. Clift
S. Battle

NFER Publishing Company

Published by the NFER Publishing Company Ltd,
Darville House, 2 Oxford Road East,
Windsor, Berks. SL4 1DF
Registered Office: The Mere, Upton Park, Slough, Berks. SL1 2DQ
© NFER
ISBN 0 85633 211 9

Typeset by Unicus Graphics Ltd, Horsham, West Sussex
Printed in Great Britain by
Staples Printers Ltd., Love Lane, Rochester
Kent ME1 1TP

Contents

Acknowledgements

The NFER research project, Parental Involvement in Primary Schools, began in September 1976 and ran for two years. It was part of a programme of research into contemporary issues in primary education and was concurrent with, and complementary to the NFER/ Schools Council Project, Record Keeping in Primary Schools. Philip Clift was Principal Research Officer, Richard Cyster was Project Leader, assisted initially by Judith Russell, and finally by Sandra Battle. Barry Sexton and Peter Smedley of NFER Statistical Services were responsible for the analysis of the data. Beulah Matthew was Project Secretary and gave invaluable support throughout, as well as typing the several drafts of the report.

The project team would like to take this opportunity to express their thanks to all those schools who took part in the project. Thanks are especially due to the head-teachers and staff of the 10 case study schools for their support and for the patience and fortitude with which they bore the team's enquiries.

NFER September 1979

Chapter 1

The New Partnership

> If we ignore or hold constant differences of personal endowment and life history, it is the interaction of homes and schools that is the key to educability. (Floud, 1956.)

> What matters most are the attitudes of teachers to parents and parents to teachers – whether there is genuine mutual respect, whether parents understand what the schools are doing for their individual children and teachers realise how dependent they are on parental support. (DES, Plowden Report, 1967.)

These quotations very aptly sum up current beliefs about the triangular partnership between children, their parents and the teachers to whom they are entrusted in their infancy.

The traditions to which present day primary education is heir are those of the elementary and preparatory schools of yester-year (Blyth, 1965). They, too, had their partnership with parents, each according to its nature and that of the social group it served. The preparatory schools were founded and maintained by public-school men: their purpose was as straight-forward as their name implies and their very existence and continued survival depended on their success in gaining places for their pupils in the prestigious public schools, attendance at which was so essential for the next generation of socially aspiring Victorian *nouveaux riches*. These parents and teachers knew precisely what the nature of their partnership was, though it was concealed to some extent by a gentlemanly facade.

In stark contrast, attendance at the public elementary school, which was the lot of most Victorian children following upon the Factory Acts, severely reduced family income and this alone may well account for the antipathy which lower class parents had for schools and teachers (Blyth, 1965, pp. 27–8). The elementary school teachers of the time, for their part, were drawn from a sector of society poised uneasily between upper working class and lower middle class. They had secured what small economic security and advantage they had by unremitting hard toil, strict moral codes and personal and family discipline and thrift. They regarded it as their bounden duty to check the habits of many of their pupils at any cost. The lower class parents were prone, with good reason, to regard teachers with contempt as,

> ... Kill-joys; sexless, tee-total prigs ..., identified with the law, the police and the 'boss class' generally, against whom they carried on a guerrilla war. The teachers, not too sure of their own authority, would reply with measures dictated by their own anxieties and lack of confidence ...

> (Highfield and Pinsent, 1952, p. 52.)

Echoes, faint or not so faint, of these traditional attitudes are heard today. During the past two years, for instance, argument and controversy have ranged over the setting up of a Parent's Charter (CASE, 1977) on the one hand, and the proper and most effective role for the Home—School Liaison worker on the other. The former reflect the efforts of mainly middle class parent pressure groups to influence the schools and the teachers, and the latter acknowledges the apathy, even antipathy, of a very different group. A further complication is the existence, even predominance in many places, of people of non-British ethnic origin and culture amongst schools' clientele.

The essentially socio-political nature of parental involvement is acknowledged in the Taylor Report, *A New Partnership for our Schools* (DES, 1977) and is clearly evident in some of the responses to it (NUT, 1978). One of its recommendations concerning the governing of schools states:

> ... The governing body should satisfy itself that adequate arrangements are made to inform parents, to involve them in their children's progress and welfare, to enlist their support, and to ensure their access to the school and teachers by reasonable arrangement. (para. 5 : 28.)

The partnership between school and community was also included in the recommendations of the Green Paper (DES, Cmnd 6869, 1977) which summarized the series of regional debates initiated by a prime-ministerial speech on education given at Ruskin College, Oxford, in 1976:

> It is an essential ingredient of this partnership that schools should be accountable for their performance: accountable to the local education authority — and those who elect it — as part of the public system of education; accountable through the school governors and managers to the local community that they serve. (para. 10:3.)

These were recommendations only, however, and the following statement contemporary with them may well be an accurate portrayal of the current situation:

> The teacher is normally insulated from the public, and from parents in particular, and is under little pressure to take account of their norms and expectations for his role. (MacIntyre, 1977.)

As with many such issues of a socio-political nature, there existed little basis of fact to inform the debate. Apart from the survey of parents' attitudes conducted for the Plowden Report, no research into the topic of parental involvement in primary schools had been undertaken to date on a *national* basis. It was to fill this gap that early in 1976 the NFER Board of Management approved a proposal to conduct a survey of parental involvement in primary schools in England and Wales. It was planned to run side by side with a project on primary school record keeping,[1] the topics being seen as to some extent complementary.

The stance of the survey was to be as neutral as possible, its main purpose being to establish the *extent and nature* of current parental involvement in the life of primary schools in England and Wales. It was specifically *not* concerned with establishing what value there might be (if any), in increasing or altering the nature of such involvement and this report therefore provides mainly descriptive rather than evaluative information. However, since it has been suggested that at least two groups of parents may be discerned — the eager and the apathetic — it is appropriate here to briefly review recent research which may suggest answers to the question, 'Why involve parents?'

---

[1] Schools Council Project: *Record Keeping in Primary Schools.* Clift, P. S., Wilson, E. L., Weiner, G. G., forthcoming publication by Schools Council.

After the passing of the 1944 Education Act, it was felt by many that the last of the institutional barriers to the 'fair society' had been removed. Children would hence-forward have access to an education appropriate to their aptitude and ability. However, it soon become apparent that children of working class origins were under-represented in the selective grammar schools, and that those who had gained entry by aptitude and ability tended to leave early. *Early Leaving* (CACE, 1954), an enquiry by the Central Advisory Council for Education, gave official recognition to the considerable influence of his home background on the child, and called for detailed investigations of the relationships between home and school. Three years later, Floud, Halsey and Martin (1957) reported that children's success in 11+ examinations varied with the material and cultural differences in their homes. Moreover, when Hertfordshire (one of the counties in which the study was conducted) abandoned selection tests, the proportion of working class boys gaining grammar school places fell, and that of middle class boys rose. This lent support to the view that the essentially middle-class ethos of the schools and teaching staff favoured the child from a similar home environment, particularly when ability to communicate verbally was being assessed.

Elizabeth Frazer's, *Home Environment and the School* (1959) can now be appreciated as a pioneer study since it attempted to determine how great was the effect of home environment on school performance, and which aspects of home environment were the most influential. Eleven items of home environment were studied, including parents' education, occupation, attitudes to education, 'abnormal' home background and family size. Four hundred Aberdeen school children from 10 schools formed the sample in 1949 and their school progress was marked and standardized to allow for variations between schools. The conclusions drawn were first that factors in the home environment were more closely correlated with school progress than with intelligence (IQ) and secondly, that the most important environmental factors were income, 'abnormal' home background and parents' attitudes to the education and future occupation of the child.

Wiseman's, *Education and Environment* (1964) largely supported Fraser's study, particularly in respect of the importance of *attitudes* as these affect the motivation of the pupil:

> The interactions of these attitudes, of child, parent and teacher, may be the greatest single force affecting the end-result of education for a particular child. It may even be argued that all other

environmental factors − school and neighbourhood − only affect educational achievement through their mediation of these attitudes. (Wiseman, 1972.)

Wiseman was, however, cautious in his interpretation of this essentially sociological perspective which emphasized the conflict of values, assumptions and aims between middle class schools and teachers, and working class children. He suggested that while many teachers were ignorant of, or even hostile to, the culture of some of their pupils this did not prevent them being efficient instructors since it was the teacher's personality and attitude toward children as individuals and learning as a progressive activity which were important (Wiseman, 1964, p. 102).

However, while it was recognized that there are wide differences in attitudes to life in general, and education in particular, found within each broad social classification, Anne Sharrock gave an 'extended treatment' to this topic in *Home School Relations* (1970) because 'it is precisely the pupils from working-class homes (however one defines working class) who may experience the greatest difficulties in school'.

The Douglas longitudinal studies of children born in England and Wales in March 1945 were unique in that they provided data on these children from birth to adulthood. *The Home and the School* (1964) provides strong evidence that between the ages of 8 and 11 children's performance in tests of mental ability and school achievement was greatly influenced by their homes and schools: 'Children from poor homes and schools deteriorate'. One factor, parents' *interest* in their childrens' school work, was statistically more significant than any of the other factors (size of family, standard of home and academic record of the school) used in this analysis. All other things being equal, the major influences on a child's ability to take advantage of educational opportunity seem to be his parent's attitudes to education and interest in his school work.

The Plowden Report (DES, 1967) re-affirmed this conclusion following analyses of data on 3,000 children and their parents. This report stands as a landmark for all those concerned in educational policy. First, it officially accepted parents as equal partners with teachers in the education of their children:

Teachers are linked to parents by the children for whom they are both responsible. The triangle should be completed and a more direct relationship established between teachers and parents.

They should be partners in more than name; their responsibility become joint instead of several. (DES, 1967, Vol. 1, p. 30.)

Secondly, it suggested a minimum programme of action by schools to involve parents as a mean of influencing parental attitudes toward education. Drawing on sociological and psychological findings with regard to the physical, mental, emotional and social (including language) development of the child, the report argued that, although genetic inheritance is fixed, interaction with the environment modifies the levels of achievement reached by the child and stated that, 'environmental factors are, or ought to be, largely within our control'. The survey data indicated that the parents' occupation, marital circumstances and education explained only about a quarter of the variation in attitudes and from this the inference was drawn that attitudes could be 'affected in other ways and altered by persuasion'. The stipulated minimum programme for all schools was one in which parents are made welcome in the school, regularly meet teachers for private talks, attend open days, receive information on the progress of their children as well as on the school's activities in general and finally receive written reports or letters at least once a year. It was further suggested that educational welfare officers should visit once a year those parents who never went near the school.

The Plowden Report recommended that the Department of Education and Science issue a booklet containing 'examples of good practice' in parent–teacher relations. The Education Survey 5 was duly published in 1968. The booklet identifies the following areas where schools could help establish better relations with parents: the points of entry (into nursery or infant classes) and subsequent school transfers, to allay fears of children and parents through adequate information and preparation; maintenance of contact with parents through regular interviews, casual encounters, visits to the classroom and more formal reports on progress; advice from LEAs to heads on encouraging parent organizations; the use of school medical and welfare services for contacting parents including the education of parents in child-rearing practices; and finally, examples of home visits made by some heads or teachers. The Plowden recommendation was taken up by others such as McGeeney who provides a more thorough account of 'good practices' found in his survey of 30 schools in *Parents are Welcome* (1969).

The Plowden Committee did not ignore the more general effect of an impoverished home, school and community environment on a child's attainment. The school was seen as one aspect of the child's environment where more immediate improvements could be made. It went further than any official body had gone before by recommending 'positive discrimination' in deprived areas, calling for the identification of 'Educational Priority Areas' (EPAs) and re-distribution and extra allocation of resources to these areas. Again parent—school relations were stressed:

> Teachers must be constantly aware that ideas, values and relationships within the school may conflict with those of the home ... There will have to be constant communication between parents and the schools if the aims of the schools are to be fully understood. (DES, 1967, Vol. 1, para. 136).

For the apathetic, or antipathetic parent then, the answer to the question, 'Why involve parents' is, 'in order to improve their children's educability'. However, to show that two things are associated does not prove that the one *causes* the other. Parents attitudes to school, and interest in their children's education are demonstrably *associated* with the children's achievement, but may not *cause* it, indeed, it may well be the other way round; that attitudes and interests are 'caused' by the achievements.

Various researchers have set out to discover whether parents' attitudes and interests 'cause' their child's school achievement, and if so in what ways.

Young and McGeeney's study, *Learning Begins at Home* (1968) began while the Plowden Committee was collecting evidence and was intended to test two of the proposals eventually contained in the Report: that positive discrimination should take place in deprived areas in order to improve education and, secondly, that parents should be more closely linked to the schools. They chose a 25 per cent sample from a junior school in London situated in a socially deprived area; the children were tested before and after researchers had initiated a programme of changes in the school. This programme involved a long letter from the head advising parents how they could help their child with school work, emphasizing the importance of attitudes, and a series of open-meetings, private talks and discussion on teaching methods held at the school. The more controversial activity of home visiting was somewhat curtailed since only three teachers were willing to undertake such visits. The researchers found that there was a slight though significant improvement in the children's scores on reading, arithmetic and non-verbal tests, but were unwilling to draw the conclusion that closer contact with parents was the cause of this rise, only that it '*could produce beneficial effects for some children*'. The analysis of the responses to the questionnaire administered to parents before the study began had shown a marked association between parental interest and educational performance but not all children with interested parents did better at school. The private talks with teachers were seen as a promising way forward, appreciated by parents and providing teachers with greater understanding of the child's background; while information pamphlets were 'one of the more obvious failures' in the initiatives taken to keep parents informed.

Also in 1968 Lawrence Green published *Parents and Teachers; Partners or Rivals?* a study of a junior school's children and parents carried out over a period of two years. This school was also situated in a poor area of an industrial city. Improvements initiated by the school included a new form of report on which parents were asked to comment and urged to come to the school to discuss their child's progress. Parents began to visit the school and others welcomed the home visits carried out by the deputy head. During the study the parents became more co-operative in their attitude toward the school and the education it provided and case studies of individual children indicated improvements in their behaviour and school performance.

It is by no means clear what it is about parents' attitudes that influences the child and there is little specific research on this but it does seem that parents *can* be influenced by action on the part of the school. Wood's doctoral thesis *Parents and the Curriculum* (1965) indicated that informing parents about what went on in school produced a swing toward viewing the curriculum more favourably than had previously been the case. However, the way this information is imparted may also be crucial. In the Schools Council's pilot study of three secondary schools *Parents and Teachers* (1976) Lynch and Pimlott found that parent discussion groups were, 'a valuable vehicle for the transmission of information about what any particular school is trying to achieve' and possibly, 'the only really satisfactory way of introducing to parents some of the more controversial proposals to improve home—school relations, such as parent attendance in classes, home-visiting by a member of the school staff and eventually the community school'. They found that parents and teachers rarely understood the concept of the community school, suggesting that it should be proceeded towards with caution and only after helping parents to become involved at a more mundane level in the school.

In these studies it is implicitly assumed that it is the parents attitudes and interests which should change. But it will be recalled that Wiseman suggested that the teacher's attitude and effectiveness as 'an instructor' was also important. Douglas' findings (1964) on the cohort of children at the primary school age had suggested that raising the standards of teaching might partly help to avoid the unequal opportunity and wasted ability that their studies had unearthed. A Canadian observational study (Hedges, 1972) of 22 elementary classes showed that when adult helpers are in the classroom the teachers allocate more time to instructing their pupils. Involving parents in this way may therefore have a more direct effect on educational opportunity than is imputed to parental attitudes.

A number of studies have been conducted on the effects of improved standards of schooling, in terms of resources, on children and parents. The policy emphasis here is on enrichment programmes, usually for pre-school age children through the expansion of nursery facilities, and positive discrimination for deprived older children. Woodhead suggested, in *Intervening in Disadvantage* (1976) that a compensatory approach of this kind often places too high an expectation on the school as an agency of social change. But he also argued against an alternative extreme tendency, to reject the relevance of conventional goals and methods for certain groups of people, preferring pragmatic solutions for the disadvantaged — defined as 'all those who fail to profit from the educational experiences made available'. His book contains a review of research in nursery education and summarizes British and American attempts at increasing parental involvement and/or education; for example, the West Riding, Home Visiting and Community Education (Red House) schemes. Here, mothers of pre-nursery age children were visited and provided with a programme designed to develop the child's skills, shown how to help their child through the programmes and hopefully later through his school years. The results indicated short-term benefits at least for the children and *potentially* greater long-term benefits due to the effects on parents. The 'Red House' project maximized contact with the community by having many facilities under one roof in an attempt to increase home–school links.

The American 'Head Start' programme gave rise to fierce and often acrimonious debate as to the value of such compensatory education when judged against the criterion of children's performance in school. 'Head Start' data provide extremely interesting insights into the value of parental involvement for parents themselves. The American educational scene is rather different from that in Britain, since American schools have always been locally controlled through an elected board, though parental activity there, as here, has largely been relegated to helping and encouraging their children. Although the British parent is responsible in law for the education of his child, this responsibility is discharged simply by sending the child to a school. However, government mandate has called on the American parent for 'maximum feasible participation' in the educational programmes of his child. Bromley (1972) indicated that this mandate was the second rationale for involving parents in Head Start, the first being 'rehabilitative' in its intent to help parents provide a more adequate educational environment for their children, following inferences regarding child development drawn from work with deprived children in America.

Parent participation in Head Start was broadly based: from a low-level peripheral involvement, to training and education for parents, the use of parents as paid employees and the involvement of some in planning and decision-making at every level of the programme. The study indicated that 'extensive parental participation is associated with many beneficial results for children, parents, Head Start Programmes and communities'. The best results were found where parents were highly involved in both decision-making and learning roles but the decision-making role appeared more potent and likely to affect the parents' learning role. The attitude survey had indicated no differences between 'high' and 'low' involvement parents (on the scales used to measure the value they placed on education) but the highly involved parents were more satisfied with their life, saw themselves as more successful, were happier than at the start of the programme and felt more able to influence and control events. One finding has implications for parental inolvement in the future: the Head Start programme did not seem to CREATE the involvement in the community and this community involvement decreased when they become involved in Head Start. Head Start was not successful in drawing in those with little community involvement at the start of the programme nor did it help raise the level of this involvement. Peters' article *Parents into the Mainstream* (1978) provides a useful overview of American legislation, parent power and participation.

The innovations of the EPA Projects have been well publicized by Eric Midwinter. As the Project Director for the Liverpool EPA he strongly advocated wide publicity for the 'zealous and imaginative work of these schools' (*Home and School Relations in Educational Priority*

Areas, 1970) and took this further in *Education For Sale* (1977). The Liverpool team successfully used local shops and pubs for displays of school work, experimenting until the best type of publications were found for describing the work of the school; an example of taking the school 'out' into the community.

So much then for the reasons for wishing to increase the involvement of the 'apathetic' parent. The evidence is that there is an association between parental interest in and attitude towards education and children's achievements in school. That it *causes* the children's achievements is less certain. What is certain is that ambitious and comprehensive attempts to involve parents in school involve increased effort on the part of head teachers and staff, who are often required to work outside the designated school hours. A good illustration of this is provided by the Glossop Gamesley Pre-School Centre (Brennan, 1974) an experimental unit set up in 1973 under Phase 3 of the Urban Aid Programme and providing nursery education and day care facilities from 8 until 5.30 each day. The head teacher and matron were available to listen to mothers' problems and encourage them to take part in the activities which included a sewing circle on one evening a week.

Turning to the eager parent, the question, 'Why involve parents' perhaps takes on a slightly querulous note. Teachers may welcome the occasional coffee morning but are wary of going into full partnership where the parent becomes a participant. Midwinter does not underestimate the teachers' fears of being swamped by parents; open to criticism while on public view and mindful of their professional status. But he argues forcefully that it is foolish, on educational grounds, to ignore parents as potential aides in the education of their children or to persist in seeing education as narrowly confined to the hours spent in school. Education on his terms is 'a dimension of life' and changes are required if it is to be seen as such. He vividly underlines the counterproductive 'bad practice' found in some schools which: 'quite consciously deploy what overtly appear as promising home–school plans to corral or contain parental hopes and aspirations ... there is the parent–teacher association deliberately manipulated by the head to avoid what he regards as possible confrontation ... A mute coolie with a full wallet would seem to be some heads' image of the perfect parent'. The involvement of parents in the school curriculum is seen by some as the most demanding and potentially profitable area of parental involvement (Wood and Simpkins, 1976). But the teacher has traditionally held a personal and autonomous influence over what is or is not taught.

The Schools Council study, *Purpose, Power and Constraint in the Primary School Curriculum* (1974) reported that in the classroom the teacher has considerable *de facto* influence while in the school the head with his *de jure* power has the most influence; that schools are not agreed about the ordering of aims and teachers do not see much advantage in stating them precisely anyway. The implication is that a teacher is in an ambiguous position, not being accountable to his clients for what he teaches nor having been granted the right to decide what is taught since this is the head's prerogative.

This may underly the closing of ranks which occurs when innovations are called for. The National Union of Teachers' reply to the Taylor Report is that increased powers for school governors is; 'impracticable, unworkable and educationally undesirable', notwithstanding the increased power in relation to the head that the recommendations would give to teachers as well as to parents in the organization of their schools. There are clearly many issues raised by parental involvement and it is hoped that the following survey data and case study material provide information on what parents, teachers and school heads perceive as important. Children's opinions of whether they want mums and dads in their school are rarely sought. Anne Garvey's survey for *Where?* (1977) provides some insight. She asked children their views and found that the younger children liked the idea: 'a parent was a status symbol to share with other children'; the 7-year-olds found it hard to grasp the full implications of having parents in school; it was: 'a strange and somewhat threatening notion' but enthusiasm built up in its favour during discussion; the children at 11 were more ambivalent in that they saw parents as frequently ignorant of, for example, modern maths and not likely to be of much help. Fee-paying parents were seen by their children as having an inalienable right to know what was going on while state educated children tended to speak less of rights while distinguishing the differences in status between parents and teachers in the matter of education, another interesting echo of tradition. Goodacre (1970) explored these 'images' of teachers and parents. Drawing on her own and other research she suggests that 'because of the somewhat isolated nature of their profession, teachers have an over-simplified, stereotyped and out-of-date image of parents'; parents, particularly the poorly educated, may be humbled and over-deferential in the face of the teacher's image as the professional educator. Again, whether or not these perceptions are accurate, they play a significant part in circumscribing the relationships between teacher and parent and are relevant when teacher and parent are required to come into closer contact and adopt new ways of viewing education.

Researchers and educational theorists have demonstrated the desirability of promoting parents' interest in their children's education, but many of the problems associated with improving home—school relationships and raising the levels of parental involvement in schools still remain to be surmounted. It is against a background of increasing concern on the part of educationists to improve home—school links, on the part of some parents to gain influence over school affairs. and on the part of teachers to preserve their professional integrity that this research study must be interpreted.

Chapter 2

Survey, Sample and Case Study

The purpose of this study was to establish the extent and nature of parental involvement in primary school life a decade after the publication of the Plowden Report. The method adopted was survey by postal questionnaire addressed to the head-teachers of a national sample of primary schools, followed by 10 case studies in which the views of assistant teachers and parents were also canvassed.

Questionnaires have a number of inherent disadvantages, mainly concerned with the quality and range of information which they provide. As to quality, there is a well known tendency for people completing questionnaires to do so in such a way as to show themselves in a good light. Known as a 'positive response set', this tendency is present to some extent whatever the means of gathering information used: people being observed are generally on their best behaviour, as are people being interviewed. A skilled researcher may be able to make *some* allowance for this when face to face, but the respondent to a questionnaire is free to portray himself as he will.

The range of information obtained is directly related to the length of the questionnaire, which in turn is inversely related to the recipients' willingness to complete and return it. There is thus a delicate balance to be struck between asking too much and getting too few responses, and severely limiting the range of information obtained by curtailing the number of questions asked.

These disadvantages have been well rehearsed elsewhere and acquaintance with them is acknowledged. The one obvious advantage of the questionnaire as a research tool is its cheapness and the size of the sample from which information may be sought.

The process by which a questionnaire is developed is also well documented. It consists of wide consultation and trial; consultation in order to ensure that it is complete as possible (one cannot have answers to questions which are not asked) and trial to ensure that its wording is clear and unambiguous. It is thus *not* undertaken in the confines of an office.

Questionnaire development began in this study with visits to a number of primary schools already familiar to the researchers. In each, the involvement of parents was discussed informally and notes were taken of what was said. This expanded considerably on the ideas about the topic which had been put forward in the original proposal. Twenty schools in three different local authorities were then visited. These 'second round' schools had been nominated by their Primary Schools Advisers as being notable for the ways in which they involved parents and were not previously known to the researchers. Interspersed with this was consultation with the representatives of various organizations with a known interest in the subject: the National Union of Teachers, The National Association of School Masters and Union of Women Teachers, The National Association of Head-teachers, the Home and School Council, and the National Confederation of Parent Teacher Associations.

. These visits resulted in a very considerable ramification of the issues involved, under two broad heads; conditions influencing parental involvement, and quantity and variety of parental involvement. They also resulted in the decision to address the questionnaire to head-teachers only, and not also to their assistants. There was one main reason for this decision. It is a well established fact that the head-teacher, particularly in a primary school, has total *de jure* power at the *school* level, and it is at this level, of policy and practice, that decisions about parental involvement, extent and type are made. The visits had confirmed this (if any confirmation was needed). At the end of this period a rough form of questionnaire existed ready for piloting.

Whilst this process of consultation and questionnaire development had been going on, the sample of schools to which the questionnaire was to be sent was drawn. The visits had also strengthened the belief held at the outset, that in respect of parental involvement, the different categories of primary school (nursery, infant, etc.) behave in somewhat different ways. It was therefore decided that the sample of schools to which the questionnaire would be sent should be drawn in such a way that parental involvement might be analysed by school type, as well as for primary schools as a collective whole, and reported at these two levels accordingly with due reference to statistically significant differences between types where they occurred.

The confidence with which data from a sample may be extrapolated to the population which it represents is determined by the *absolute size* of the sample. Thus the number of schools drawn in each category was determined not by their relative proportions as primary schools, but by the decision at the outset to aim for certain confidence limits for each; that is, to be 95 per cent confident that the sample data would reflect that of the totality in each category within a specifiable range plus or minus of the reported (i.e., sample response) figure. The samples drawn in the first instance were in accordance with the categorization of primary schools made available by the Department of Education and Science.

Nursery	(15%)
JMI Infant or First school with nursery unit	(15%)
Infant or First school without nursery unit	(8%) †
JMI, or Combined without nursery unit	(4%)
Junior, or Middle school deemed primary	(8%)

(† of all such schools in England and Wales)

The second category was subsequently 'split' into infant and first school with nursery unit, and JMI or combined primary with nursery unit, for greater accuracy and ease of interpretation of data. It had not been possible to achieve this finer categorization on the basis of information available at the time of sampling. It was subsequently done by using the responses to Question 1 in the questionnaire (Appendix (i)) which asked about school type. When data from the different categories of primary school were subsequently aggregated, it was of course necessary to first weight it so that the contribution of each category was proportionately correct.

Permission to seek the co-operation of each school was then sought from their Chief Education Officer. A copy of the pilot form of the questionnaire accompanied the letter in order to show clearly the purposes of the exercise and how demanding of head-teacher's time it was likely to be. Permission was given in all cases. (This step by step account is given here because a number of heads expressed curiosity as to how they had come to be included, and it may well be that others might also wish to know.)

A sub-sample of 170 (approximately 10 per cent) of the aggregate sample were sent a copy of the pilot questionnaire along with a letter explaining its purpose and state of development and seeking their help in its refinement. Specifically what was sought was an indication of:

(i) its completeness (was there any aspect of parental involvement and home—school relationship as understood, not included?);

(ii) its ambiguities;

(iii) the range of response.

Regarding the last, many of the questions were open-ended at this stage; that is, space had been left for the head-teacher to write in his own answer. The analysis of 100 or 200 such questionnaires is feasible, but the task becomes too time-consuming when thousands are involved. The answers given were listed and categorized in order to provide the sets of alternatives amongst which the respondents could select in the final version.

About 75 per cent of head-teachers responded at this stage. In spite of the earlier discussions, a number of matters not previously introduced were brought up by this piloting. One such was a general insistence on referring to the 'problems' heads had experienced in dealing with parents, and a section on this was included in the final version.

The version finally sent to the main sample was agreed after visits to 12 of the pilot schools. It still included one or two open-ended questions, notably one where the researchers had been advised of an ethical objection to asking teachers to agree to certain statements. It was accepted that to do so was 'putting words in teachers' mouths', but it is interesting to reflect that when replies from the main sample came in they almost all fell within the response set indicated by the pilot schools.

The final draft of the questionnaire, which is included as Appendix (i), was sent to the main sample of 1,700 schools at the beginning of the summer term, 1977 and, following the sending of a reminder letter, a response rate of over 80 per cent was attained, not counting those that arrived too late for inclusion in the analysis. This reply is unusually high for this type of research and lends added credence to the results obtained.

At the same time as the final drafts were sent to the schools, a copy was sent to each Chief Education Officer together with a letter asking for information about their *policy* regarding parental involvement in primary schools. Seventy per cent of them replied, and the information they supplied was used to determine whether policy was reflected in action in schools.

With the coding and analysis of the questionnaire completed, the second stage of the project was approached. A number of schools which had given interesting responses were visited, both to help with the formulation of ideas as to the form the case-studies should take, and to investigate with the head-teachers the possibility of the continued inclusion of their schools in the research. After consultation with a number of head-teachers a three-fold approach was adopted:

(1) observation of teachers, and where appropriate parents, at work in the classroom situation;
(2) semi-structured interviews with both teaching and non-teaching staff;
(3) semi-structured interviews with a 10 per cent sample of parents, chosen at random from the school registers.

The purpose of the observation constituent was to provide a 'setting', highlighting areas of concern for inclusion in the interview schedules and to enable the results of these interviews to be more accurately interpreted. The teacher interviews formed the main thrust of the case-studies. They were used to investigate the type and extent of parental involvement in each school and teachers' views as to the value of this involvement for themselves, the parents and the relationship between them. Interviews with parents provided the essential complement to these, allowing the different perceptions of school held by those 'on the outside' to be discerned.

Case studies were made of 10 schools. This was felt to be the maximum number in which the project team could satisfactorily complete the research, given the time and resources available. With one exception the schools finally chosen for case study were those in which interesting forms of parental involvement were being attempted. The exception was made to allow for a comparative study (see Chapter 9). The schools involved covered the whole primary age range (3–11 years) and were widely geographically dispersed. They comprised two nurseries, two infant schools, one first school, one junior school and four JMI schools, all with nursery classes. Six of the schools were situated in urban areas and the rest in small towns or villages, in north-west and south-west England, the Midlands, the Home Counties and London. About two dozen schools were approached in the first instance and both head-teachers and their staff were fully briefed as to the nature and objectives of the research before their cooperation was sought and, in 10 cases, enlisted. The major characteristics of the case study schools are set out in Table 2 :1.

N.B. *All names of schools, teachers, pupils and parents are of course fictitious.*

It is not claimed that results obtained from these case study schools can be generalized to cover the whole range of primary schools. The study of home–school relations in microcosm may, however, be used to illuminate the quantitative data, obtained by questionnaire from a representative sample, and provide a necessary supplement of more qualitative data that the questionnaire was not designed to elicit.

Instrumental in gaining the cooperation of head-teachers of case study schools was the project's willingness to offer something in return for their help. Since an important constituent of the research involved canvassing the views of a random sample of parents, the heads were offered a summary of their views as expressed, hopefully, 'without fear or favour', to the project team. Since schools generally encounter the real feelings of only the relatively biased sample of parents who become involved in the Parent Teacher Association or who help out at the annual jumble sale, this was a strong 'selling point', representing as it did an excursion into educational consumer research at a time when consumers, both in education and out of it, are being championed by ever more powerful pressure-groups.

As stated earlier, the selection of parents for interview was random, taking every tenth child from the school registers. In all the schools many families were represented by more than one child; this led to over-sampling and helped to maintain sample size when interviews were refused or parents proved impossible to contact. Head-teachers were consulted about those children selected and occasionally, at their suggestion, adjustments to the lists were made to take account of family difficulties (in one tragic case, the death by drowning of the selected child).

It was considered important to inform all parents at the selected schools about the research being carried out, both to minimize the effects of any gossip that might start and to enable those parents who, though not chosen for interview, still wished to make their views known, to do so. A second letter was sent out to sample parents a few days before the project team were scheduled to be in the area con-

Table 2.1: Characteristics of the case study schools

School	No. of Pupils on Roll	School Architecture	School Organization	School Location
Riverside Nursery	60 part-time	Part of an old converted house.	Informal nursery.	Small Home Counties' market town. Prosperous area but many parents 'deprived'.
Mill Street Nursery	80 full-time	Bottom floor of a large converted secondary school.	Informal within general timetable.	Inner-city area in west Midlands. Racially mixed and economically deprived catchment area.
Blenheim Infants	90	Traditional, closed-plan redbrick school.	Class teaching with partial vertical grouping and integrated day.	Greater London. Urban area with skilled or semi-skilled parent population.
Elm Road Infants	150	Open-plan with three classroom areas.	Cooperative teaching, integrated day and partial vertical grouping.	Small Home Counties town. Working-class catchment area with a number of Italian immigrants.
Brunel First	200	Large, closed-plan building. Extra space available for group work.	Traditional classroom teaching. Horizontally grouped classes.	Large Home Counties town. Working-class council estate catchment area.
Barchester Junior	380	Traditionally designed, new building, classroom based with space available for group work.	Traditional teaching approach. Horizontally grouped classes setted for basic subjects.	Outskirts of city in west of England. Lower middle-class private housing estate catchment area.
Tyler Primary	300	Older infants, new juniors, both open-plan classrooms provided for group work.	Team-teaching, integrated day approach, partial vertical grouping.	West Midlands industrial city. Very deprived low-rise council estate catchment area.
Carford Primary	480	Large semi-open-plan converted secondary. School hall and nursery unit.	Cooperative or team-teaching: infants partially vertically grouped integrated day. Junior horizontally grouped traditional day.	Market town in west of England. Working-class, newly erected council estate catchment area.
St Hilda's Primary	200	New, closed-plan building with integral nursery unit.	Horizontally-grouped class teaching. Integrated day approach.	Schools situated within one mile of each other in old established, working-class council estate on outskirts of large city in north-west England. Both schools Roman Catholic.
Spiritus Sanctus Primary	200	Old, closed-plan building with integral nursery unit. One spare classroom.	Horizontally-grouped class teaching. Traditional teaching approach.	

cerned, advising parents to expect a visit and again explaining the nature of the research being carried out.

Interviews were conducted in parents' own homes, this being considered the place in which they would feel most at ease. As less than a quarter of all parents visited had telephones, this entailed much knocking on doors before even appointment for interviews could be made. Surprisingly few refusals were met with, and the welcome given was encouragingly warm. Just occasionally there was some initial suspicion that the researchers were in fact either from the local education authority 'sent to check up on them', or alternatively attempting by ever more devious means to sell encyclopedias.

Teacher interviews were, by and large, much easier to conduct as more common ground existed between teacher and interviewer. It was also possible to tape-record the majority of these interviews whereas any attempt to do so with parents might well have engendered a deep suspicion of motives, if not open hostility.

All field-work was completed shortly after Easter 1978, the last four months of the project being devoted to writing this report.

Chapter 3

Head-teachers' Perceptions of Parental Involvement

In its final form the questionnaire fell neatly into two parts. The first dealt with characteristics of the school thought likely to have a significant influence on the amount and type of parental involvement. These characteristics had been cited during the development of the questionnaire as being of importance in the schools visited, and by those completing the pilot version. The second part dealt with the variety of forms which involvement might take. Thus the first section contained questions on school age, size and staffing, architecture and curriculum and the general school environment. The second section contained questions asking about Parent Teacher Associations, open evenings, fund raising, parents helping in school and the associated problems, as well as a number of other varieties of parent–school contact. A copy of the questionnaire is included as Appendix (i).

The 83 per cent response rate to the questionnaire was considered to be highly satisfactory. The rate for each school type in the sample is shown in Table 3.1.

For the first three categories the response was very high indeed, which may indicate how important these respondents judge this topic to be.

The response rate for the last two categories is noticeably lower than that for the others. This seems to be related to the age of the children and the weaker 'natural' link with parents which schools for older children have because the parents no longer bring their children to school.

Table 3.1: Response rate for each school type

School Type	Questionnaires sent out		returned		Res-
	% of population	Number	% of population	Number	ponse rate, %
Nursery school	15	104	13.5	93	89
JMI, infant or first school with nursery unit	15	348	14.6	339	97
Infant or first school without nursery unit	8	387	7.1	344	89
JMI or combined without nursery unit	4	458	2.9	332	73
Junior or middle school	8	395	5.9	293	74
Total		1,692		1,401	83

As discussed earlier (p. 24) this initial sampling frame of five categories of school was subsequently expanded to six to form Question 1 of the questionnaire, the second category being 'split' into infant or first school with nursery unit (213 respondents) and JMI with nursery unit (126 respondents).

It had been hypothesized that parental involvement would differ significantly by school type, and in particular that nursery schools, and schools with nursery classes would involve parents to a greater extent than other schools catering for children of primary school age. In order to test this hypothesis, school type (Question 1) was cross-tabulated with the section of the questionnaire which asked about involvement (Question 9–12). The results of these cross-tabulations are presented as Appendix (ii), and are discussed throughout this chapter, first for primary schools as a whole,[1] then, where differences amongst the different types of primary school are such as to reach the 0.001 level of statistical significance, for each type separately.

Surprisingly, only 35 per cent of all primary schools have a Parent Teacher Association (PTA) or other formal parent association. Even when added to the 26 per cent who claim a less formal parents' committee or 'Friends of the School', this leaves about 40 per cent

---

[1] See notes on tables at the beginning of Appendix (ii).

without any parent group recognizable as such. However, this represents a distinct increase on the findings of the survey carried out for
the Plowden Report (DES, 1967) when only 17 per cent of primary
schools had a Parent Teacher Association.

As expected, PTAs are far less common in schools catering for the
lower end of the age-range where the need for such formal liaison is
more likely to be diminished by the day-to-day contact between
teachers and parents. The relationship between school type and
presence of a PTA is statistically significant.

The relationship between school type and presence of less formal
parents' committees is not significant, although their presence at junior
or middle schools is noticeably less marked. It is possible that for
many schools, and in particular nurseries, a formal or informal parents
association is not considered the most effective method of creating a
home—school link.

The aims of parent teacher associations, whether formal or informal
do not differ significantly between school type. The most common are:
to provide a close link between home and school (56 per cent) and to
raise funds (55 per cent). Fifty-one per cent of primary schools see such
associations as being important in giving parents and teachers a better
understanding of each other's problems. Forty-two per cent consider
that it should inform parents of the school's teaching methods and
educational philosophy and 39 per cent that it should provide a point
of contact with the local community.

In fact, a number of head-teachers, both at the case study schools
and at others visited, said that a formal PTA would just 'scare parents
away'. The head of Tyler Primary (a case study school) explained:

> Since most of our parents were school failures initially, we need
> to establish confidence. We need to break down old prejudices
> and attitudes to school. We then need to give parents confidence
> in what they can offer.

The head of Mill Street nursery (another case study school) was
also concerned to build up parents' self-confidence:

> In fact we have to reassure them that they are their children's
> first teachers and as such must accept their responsibilities. So
> really we offer a supportive role towards the parents and in turn
> they support us.

Both heads were convinced that their parents would be totally unable to deal with any expression of home–school contact so formal as a PTA.

Other arguments were advanced against PTAs at other schools visited. The head of an infant school in a racially mixed urban area said:

> We have no formal PTA because in an area like this with only a few white parents, I feel it could easily become dominated by them. That is why I wouldn't want any sort of formal or structured situation.

The head of an infant school in a deprived area of an outer London borough expressed similar sentiments:

> My aim is to make *everyone* believe that they have something to contribute to the school – which is why in this school I will not have a PTA. PTAs are run by a committee and I know full well that if we had one here most of my parents would say, 'what is the use of my offering to do anything, the committee will do it all?'. Everyone is welcome here – and do as much or as little as they are able. In some cases parents have very little time, but at least they know they are always welcome in this school – and I believe this is the reason that so many parents support everything we do in the school.

In schools where PTAs were established, their activities were often restricted to the raising of money and the organizing of social events. The head of a large middle school in the Home Counties said:

> All our parents are involved in that they are members of the PTA automatically. We abolished subs, right at the start, so no-one is excluded on financial grounds. We elect a committee to plan a year's activities and I discuss with the staff what we would like to achieve in that year and the PTA helps up to reach our goal. (The PTA have by their money-raising efforts purchased a coach, a mini-bus, an indoor swimming pool as well as large quantities of books and audio-visual equipment.)
>
> I see the PTA as being a service to the school, serving if you like the needs of their children. This is especially valuable at a time when money is short in the country and PTA funds can be used to see that our equipment is maintained at a high level. I don't see the PTA as having any say in the running of the school.

Ninety-two per cent of schools invite new parents to visit them before their children start to attend. This practice is significantly related to school type, however, being less prevalent in junior and middle schools (74 per cent). Head-teachers see this as a valuable introduction to the school and its methods for both parent and child. The head of Elm Road infants explained:

> The children are invited in for at least an hour, and more usually a whole morning, to stay in the classroom before they come into school.

Sixty-six per cent of schools send written information about themselves to new parents. This is again significantly related to school type, being generally less common in schools for younger children, suggesting that it is seen as the counter-part of the introductory visits favoured by these schools. There is clear indication in the figures that the presence of a nursery class *reduces* the likelihood of a school sending written information to new parents. This is understandable if, as hypothesized, nursery classes enjoy an 'automatic' and more immediate relationship between home and school.

Many heads to whom the pilot questionnaire was sent returned with it copies of newsletters, booklets, etc., sent out to new and prospective parents. They varied in approach and format depending on the school and its area, but nearly all gave information on the school timetable, dress requirements, availability of the head to see parents and arrangements for swimming, games or school trips. A minority also included details of methods used to teach language and number and listed ways in which parents might help their children in their school work at home. One or two heads argued that if parents were going to help their children at home anyway, they would far rather they followed the same methods as the school; thus the inclusion of details of teaching techniques.

Methods of Involvement

Parents are invited to attend open days or open evenings at 97 per cent of all primary schools. This practice is again significantly related to school type, with far fewer nursery schools (74 per cent) doing so. In 52 per cent of all schools open days or evenings take place once or twice a year, though in nursery schools they are generally held once a term. In 85 per cent of schools over half of the parents attend on these occasions. Level of attendance is significantly related to school type.

Open days take a number of forms, the most usual of which appears to be the presentation for parents of a harvest festival celebration and/or a Christmas nativity play. Next in popularity are formal discussions between parents and teachers about children's school work (87 per cent) and, summer fetes and sports days (85 per cent), displays of children's work (84 per cent), exhibitions of project work involving the class or even the whole school (53 per cent) invitations into the classroom to see the children at work (43 per cent), and prize days (10 per cent). All are significantly related to school type, generally increasing with the increase in the age of children catered for by the school. The exception is that parents are more likely to be invited into the classroom to see their children at work in nursery schools and in schools with nursery classes.

The approach of the case study schools to open days varied. The head of Carford primary reported:

> We've only been open just over a year but we're establishing a pattern of parents in school. We've had three social evenings so far;... On the formal side we have 'come and look at Johnnie's work' evenings. We have two lots a year; one just after the the children have started in September or October so that the teacher is able to get from mum or dad any home problems; then later on, towards the end of the year, mum and dad can come along and have another chat with the teacher.

The head of Spiritus Sanctus explained the importance of supplementing the twice yearly ration of formal open evenings with other opportunities for parent—school contact:

> There must be opportunities to talk to individual parents. I am not quite sure how you do this. Five minutes twice a year does not seem very satisfactory, especially if you have to wait with other parents for 25 minutes just to talk to the teacher for five. On the other hand, talking to 30 or 40 parents just for five minutes is a very demanding process for the teacher.
>
> If you are concerned abour your child as an individual and his treatment in the school generally or by one teacher in particular I don't think you should have to wait until the next parents' evening.

As far as parents visiting schools to see their children at work was concerned, the head of Elm Road infants reported some of the difficulties this could lead to:

We did try this. This can be a little overwhelming for the teachers and for the children... In a previous school I worked in, they came *en masse.* They were invited for the afternoon and at the end of the afternoon I was going to give them a little talk; it worked too well because we were so swamped with parents that it just wasn't a normal afternoon in school. Parents just didn't see the school working normally because we were too overwhelmed by the number of adults around and you couldn't conduct a normal classroom situation.

Apart from open days, almost all schools (98 per cent) make provision for parents to discuss their children's work or problems by appointment with the teachers or the head. This practice is also significantly related to school type, with fewer nursery schools (80 per cent) making, or perhaps needing to make, this form of provision. In 95 per cent of schools, parents visit when they want to discuss a particular problem. In rather fewer schools (67 per cent) they are specifically invited by the head or their child's teacher. This practice occurs in only 32 per cent of nursery schools. In fewer schools still (31 per cent) parents visit irregularly, 'just to check up on things'.

Informal contact between parents and school is also very common; in 91 per cent of schools parents stop to chat with the teacher when leaving their children at school in the morning and picking them up in the afternoon. Understandably, this practice is significantly less common at junior and middle schools (68 per cent). In almost all schools (96 per cent) parents 'drop in' to see the head when they feel the need arises and this is equally true for all school types. In 56 per cent of schools parents are invited to visit teachers and/or the head at the end of the school day. This practice is significantly less frequent in nursery schools (37 per cent).

Informal contact with parents was considered by the head-teachers of all the case study schools to be very important. This is the means by which the foundations of good parent—teacher relationships are laid. At infant and nursery schools contact is most often made in the morning when parents bring their children to school and in the afternoon when they collect them. The headmistress of Elm Road infants reported:

In this school, really, parents come and go quite freely. They bring their children in in the morning, they see them settling down to the classroom situation. They collect them again at the end of the afternoon, so parents do see quite a lot of what is going on in school and we manage to get to know them, which I think is most important.

The deputy-head at Mill Street nursery agreed and also explained why parents stayed on at the nursery to help:

Well, in the beginning, of course, they have to come in, whether they like it or not, to settle the children. Even when they've settled their child, they still have to bring the child into the classroom in the morning and say, 'good morning' to the headmistress so that she knows they have arrived. They take them to the member of staff responsible for their child and say 'good morning' to them and at night the same process is repeated so we know which children gave gone and which are still here. So basically, they have to come in, but really it's such a nice atmosphere here, and we've always made the parents very welcome. Once you've said, 'hello' to them, some of them are very shy and rush off straight away but others might like to stop and pass the time of day for five minutes. Then later on, when you've got to know them a bit better, they might start talking about the children and they might actually want to ask you something so they'll stop and talk to you.

All head-teachers in the case study schools made efforts to convince parents, especially new parents, that they could see them at any time if they had a problem or something they wanted to discuss. The head of Spiritus Sanctus said:

At least twice a year parents come in and talk to the teachers but very often when I write to parents about things that are happening in school I repeat the open invitation to them to come in whenever they have any cause for concern, or even if they haven't and just want to come in and talk to me.

Almost 70 per cent of primary head-teachers estimated that they or their staff see over half of their pupils' parents in a year to discuss the children's schooling. The proportion of parents seen is significantly related to school type, decreasing with the increase in age of the children.

The large numbers of head-teachers (80 per cent) who discuss parents' social or marital problems with them is surprising. A question on this had been inserted following discussions during the piloting and drafting of the questionnaire with a number of heads who had reported that their time was being increasingly taken up in 'counselling' parents on non-educational matters. It was the high response to this question that prompted its inclusion as part of the teacher interview schedule for the case study schools. It is significantly related to school type, being appreciably more common in nursery schools (93 per cent) than in JMIs without nurseries (73 per cent).

Mrs Askew, the headmistress of Riverside nursery, explained that for her, educating the child went hand in hand with educating and if necessary helping the parent. She explained the role the nursery could play in this:

> I always stress that the atmosphere in a nursery must be secure, happy and loving. A mother with problems will thrive in such an atmosphere because if she does feel inadequate, what she is also lacking is love and that we can provide in the nursery by caring enough about her as a person. Because the nursery environment is happy and secure it's a smashing place to bring these mums so they can learn to relax and enjoy their children.

The need to provide a responsible and caring milieu for both parents and children was also recognized by the head of St Hilda's primary. Asked if he considered it part of his job to counsel parents, he replied:

> If we care enough we'll do everything else right anyway, so I don't neglect the counselling part, I'm always available for parents from 8.30 to 9.00 and they can come any lunchtime, though I'm not always in. I'm always here after school so that parents have free access to me. For instance, the woman next door, she was having trouble with her husband and she fled in here one morning because he was beating her up and this was her only refuge, her only haven; I couldn't turn her out, could I? Then the counselling started as a result of that. But I do see counselling as part of my function here. If we have a policy on parents it must be part of it.

The head of Elm Road infants also spent time in dealing with parents' problems:

> Well, I think as head of a school that it is inevitable that this happens. Parents come in and ask anyway, and in a situation where you are working in a social priority school you find that you are somebody who is used just as a sympathetic ear. Parents come in and tell me their problems and they just sit and talk and this is what they need to do, talk it out with somebody, somebody who is sympathetic and will listen. But apart from that I have had parents coming in asking for advice for a number of

> reasons. Recently we had a child whose father had just left home and the mother was terribly distressed; she couldn't get her little boy to come to school in the morning, and she asked me what on earth she could do and how she could resolve the situation. This is the sort of situation you get... I have no particular ruling about when they come because I think these parents need to come when they have a problem, especially if it's a particularly pressing problem. I know it's hard on me and it makes my job difficult but I never refuse to see a parent here and I always tell them that I'll be available if it's pressing'

The role taken by the schools in the advising and counselling of parents will be dealt with more fully in Chapter 7.

Parents help with fund-raising in almost all primary schools (96 per cent). The most popular form appears to be jumble sales, summer fetes, bazaars, etc. (87 per cent), and the least popular dances or parties (42 per cent). The funds raised are very rarely devoted solely to charity or used solely by the parents themselves. In 33 per cent of primary schools they are used as contributions to the school fund, but in the majority (61 per cent) they are put to a mixture of uses. The relationship between the uses of funds raised and school type is statistically significant. Over half of the parents are involved in fund-raising in 80 per cent of primary schools.

Parents are invited to workshop meetings to discuss the work their children do and/or methods of assessment at 34 per cent of primary schools. Most commonly (18 per cent) meetings occur when the head feels it to be necessary, and rarely (3 per cent) at the parents' request, the slight exception to this being in nursery schools. In 14 per cent of primary schools, workshops are included as part of another social event.

Two of the case-study schools held workshop meetings and one other had plans for them. The head of Blenheim infants reported on those held at her school:

> The educational evenings we had on maths and reading were very successful. The parents were amazed at the new methods. Many of them do not really understand what the new methods mean and are suspicious, since school is nothing like it was for them. We have plans for more evenings like this, where we put out our equipment and have slides to illustrate how it is used in class.

Tyler primary had also held workshop meetings, but with less encouraging results:

There was very poor attendance at a language evening two years ago, even though we published it well. The children put leaflets through the doors, put up posters and took letters home. One Community Education Officer said it was one of the best evenings of its kind that he had seen in the area but when so few come, you wonder whether it's worth the effort.

The head of St Hilda's primary, on the other hand, thought that they might be used to replace the conventional open-day for parents:

They are tired of trotting round and seeing their children's work on the walls, they've seen it before. They are very happy with the state of the school and what the kids are being taught, they have a great respect for the staff and that is very evident. That side of things is alright but we need to meet as a forum now, because the system has changed so such in the last 10 years. We need to be able to set up a classroom and say, 'come in, sit down, and see the turmoils through which your child has to travel'. One alternative to that would be every teacher running a little class for parents, or using one big classroom in the hall with all the teachers taking part as a team, followed by a talk and discussion.

Sixty-three per cent of schools explain teaching methods they use to new parents at an initial meeting. This procedure is significantly related to school type, being most frequent in infant schools without nursery classes (76 per cent). Such infant schools will, of course, generally admit 'unknown' children (as compared with 'known' children from attached nursery classes in infant schools with nursery units) in substantial batches, mainly in September and January.

School Based Involvement

Questions 10e:38–51 asked about school and class-based activities in which parents may be involved. The weighted percentages of all primary schools involving parents in the various activities specified is shown in Table 3.2 in rank order of their popularity.

Six of these forms of practical involvement are significantly related to school type in ways conforming to expectation. Thus there tends to be significantly more classroom-based involvement in schools for younger children (e.g. parents help with craft work, cooking, etc., and parents help generally in the classroom). Parental help with dressing children after swimming or physical education is also significantly more prevalent in schools for younger children. Conversely, parental help with football, etc., and with providing transport for 'away' games

Table 3.2: **Parental involvement in school-based activities**

Type of Involvement	Schools, %	Sig.
Parent help on school visits and outings	78	NS
Parents do sewing (e.g., costumes for Christmas play) and minor repairs to school equipment	65	NS
Parents provide transport for football, etc., matches matches at other schools	54	<0.001
Parents with specialist knowledge, e.g., local policeman, fireman, etc., give talks to children	45	NS
Parents help with craft work, cooking, music, etc., under supervision of teacher	36	<0.001
Parents help in school library, covering books, etc.	29	<0.001
Parents hear children read under supervision of teacher	26	NS
Parents help with football, after school clubs, etc	22	<0.001
Parents help dress children after PE or swimming	20	<0.001
Parents help generally in classroom, putting out materials cleaning up at end of day, etc.	19	<0.001
Parents do major repairs and/or alterations to school building (e.g., turn cloakrooms into classrooms)	10	NS
Parents run or help with holiday play scheme	7	NS
Parents run a library scheme for the school	4	NS

is significantly more common in schools for older children. Parental help in the school library, covering books, etc., is also significantly related to school type, being most frequent in infants' schools, where the children have generally reached the age where books play an important part in their daily lives, but are not yet perhaps, old enough to maintain them themselves.

By far the most popular types of school-based parental involvement — helping on school visits and outings, the sewing of costumes for Christmas plays, etc., and carrying out minor repairs to school equipment — are not significantly related to school type. Another popular form of parental involvement, where those with specialist knowledge give talks to the children, seems unrelated to school type. Major repairs or alterations to the school buildings by parents are relatively rare, as is parental help running a holiday play scheme, and a library scheme. Differences amongst primary schools over the vexed issue of hearing children read fail to reach the 0.001 level of statistical significance despite the fact that it hardly ever occurs in nursery schools. About one-quarter of all other types of school involve parents in this way despite the 'professional misgivings' of many teachers.

In fact the debate over parents' involvement in classroom based activities has most often focused upon the erosion of teachers' professionalism, with the teaching of reading emerging as the central issue. Though all heads to whom the team spoke agreed that parents should never be employed to 'teach' reading to non-readers or to children who were having difficulty with their reading, they were divided on the question of parents working with fluent readers. Many felt that parents hearing children read, no matter how fluent they were, still amounted to teaching and called into question the three years' professional training undergone by the class teacher. Others were more of the opinion held by the head of a primary school in an East Anglian market town:

> If we believe that a child needs a warm relationship with an adult to learn to read — then we should, if necessary, provide a surrogate mother. The bastions of tradition need undermining — why is everyone so sensitive about the fanciful differences between the hearing and teaching of reading?

Forms and amount of school based parental involvement varied widely among the case study schools. Head teachers often had strong views on activities in which it was or was not appropriate for parents to involve themselves.

Not all the head-teachers to whom the team spoke, however, were in favour of parents working in the classroom setting. The head of Spiritus Sanctus, for instance, had grave reservations:

> No, I have very strong feelings about this, I don't see how you can look after children without teaching them and if you have parents in classrooms they are in some way teaching children. First of all they usually teach them the wrong way, as they do at home and secondly, if you want them taught, then a teacher has to spend a lot of time teaching the parent how to do it. I've heard of head-teachers running courses for parents but if we want a profession, then we have to behave like a profession and you can't teach parents to be teachers in three lessons after 4 p.m. We've shouted for long enough that teachers must be properly trained and then we cut the ground from under our own feet by bringing in Mrs so-and-so, a nice lady from along the road who can do the job as

well as anybody else. You can't ask parents to come in and tidy cupboards out or sort the PE kit, it would be insulting. We have an ancillary assistant to do this sort of thing and she gets paid for it. Can you see mothers coming in and doing it for long when they see that one of them is getting paid for it?

The head of St Hilda's liked to see parents helping in the classroom providing his staff were happy with the idea:

They should only be in the classroom if teachers want them; I'm very definite about this. I won't impose any parents on any teacher, though I will encourage it. It's happened in the infants because I think it lends itself to parents, infant teaching. Briefly the sort of things that parents can do are these: they could hear them read, it's good to have a child read to an adult especially when they've conquered the early skills, when they've broken the code. Somebody must listen to them and the teacher hasn't always got the time; a good parent, any parent, can hear a child read and it's carried out then into the homes. The importance of hearing a child read can be reinforced in this way to parents. I would say that sitting, talking to a group of children is important, operating machines, setting up tape recorders, setting up language tapes where they are doing a mundane thing in a positive way; it's mundane for them, it's positive for the child. They can help the child to get over its early difficulties, not operating the system for them but being there as a helping hand.

However, there were other ways in which parents' presence in the classroom could be beneficial, and he described one particular instance in which a parent had been asked to come in to help out in her son's classroom in order to give him the security he so badly needed. The head believed the dramatic improvement in the child's self-confidence and general attitude to work fully vindicated his actions in this respect.

The head of Carford primary was also aware of the role parents could play in the school in giving a sense of security to the children:

As far as their activities in the class go, essentially they come in as a mum or a dad. Lots of our children have not got either a mum or a dad so they are able to fulfil that relationship with one child or more than one child. If you're asking for specific things that they do in school, that is number one; they come in and provide a warm friendly relationship, you can call it language development; you can call it a number of things, but I think the

main role is being there as a dad or a mum in any situation . . . I
would love to see the day when we have grannies in school
because I think they have a lot to give and it would be nice
to have working dads in the school, the local chimney sweep
coming and telling us about his day, the pigeon-fancier from
round the corner telling us about his hobby; real people that
matter coming in to school and becoming involved in what is
really an exciting adventure; that's the way I see it.

Other forms of school-based involvement reported by head-teachers
include: help with school parties (Christmas, etc.), and fetes, running a
toy library, supplying materials of various kinds for craft work, running
the school tuckshop, and running a mothers' club and mother and
toddler groups.

To sum up, there is little evidence to support the hypothesis that
levels of parental involvement are generally higher in nursery schools
or in schools with nursery classes, though classroom based activities
involving parents appear to occur more frequently in schools catering
for the lower age-ranges.

Problems Associated with the Involvement of Parents

Questions 10f:52–65 dealt with the problems encountered by
primary schools in attempting to involve parents. Table 3.3 lists these
questions together with the weighted combined percentage of primary
schools reporting these problems as significant (s) and minor (m), and
whether there are statistically significant differences amongst the
different types of primary schools in respect of each.

The problem which appears to face most primary schools is that of
actually involving parents at all. In more than half of all schools,
mothers being out at work, hence unavailable during the school day, is
seen as a problem of a greater (25 per cent) or lesser (28 per cent)
degree. There is a statistically significant relationship between this
problem and school type, nursery schools being less affected.

The head of Elm Road infants (a case study school) said:

> I think lack of support, apathy, ignorance very often, not under-
> standing what we are trying to do and why. It's sad too to see
> children's faces when their parents don't turn up for school
> assemblies or to other activities they are invited to. They are
> forgetful too and we have to send out constant reminders. With
> our immigrant families, of course, we have the problems of lack
> of communication because they don't understand our letters, but
> we do have the help of an excellent educational welfare officer
> who will liaise for us.

Table 3.3: **Problems associated with parental involvement**

Problems	Problem rating	% of schools	Sig.
Lack of confidentiality on the part of some parents, e.g., parents gossiping between each other about some children's inability to read, their bad behaviour, etc.	S* M	7 25	NS
Presence of parents in classroom causes behaviour problems in children	S M	4 14	< 0.001
Complaints from those parents not involved about those who are	S M	3 10	NS
Staff unwilling to allow parents into their classroom	S M	8 15	NS
Parents unreliable in the time and amount they turn up to help	S M	5 13	NS
Parents too eager, try to take over class from teachers or school from head	S M	3 4	NS
Parents more interested in their own child than the class as a whole	S M	7 19	NS
Parents do not fully understand the aims of the school, so tend to criticize what teachers do	S M	3 15	NS
Parents wish to help in the school for the wrong reasons, e.g., because they are bored at home	S M	3 11	NS
Parents apathetic, unwilling to take the least interest in school and its activities	S M	8 21	< 0.001
Many of the mothers working so they cannot come into the school to help	S M	25 28	< 0.001
Problems in attracting parents who either can't or don't want to visit the school	S M	18 28	NS
Problems of involving parents who have difficulty in speaking English	S M	7 8	< 0.001
Others: please specify	S M	3 2	NS

* S = significant problem; M = minor problem.

Just under one-half of all schools encounter the related problem of attracting parents who are either unable or unwilling to visit at any time (18 per cent significant and 28 per cent minor).

The problem most frequently cited as significant by nursery schools is that of parents who have difficulty in speaking English. This is probably explained by the prevalence of classroom based parental involvement in such schools and the strong possibility that their priority intake would include non-English-speaking children.

Parental unreliability in respect of undertakings to help is cited as a problem in just under one-fifth of primary schools (5 per cent significant, 13 per cent minor).

The head of Mill Street nursery found that parents were often unreliable about turning up to help:

> No matter how good they are and how much they want to help, in an area like this they are not very reliable. You can't rely on them to come in at any particular time and at the most crucial moment they might let you down. There are others where the child is not ready to cope with sharing his mother's attention with 60 other children. There are very good people who will be very helpful but they have to wait till the child has got to the stage when he couldn't care less whether his mother is there or not. In an area like this responsibility falls on a very few people and we couldn't rely on having the school open with just parents helping.

The presence of parents in the classroom is seen as a cause of behaviour problems in children by just under one-fifth of primary schools (4 per cent significant, 14 per cent minor), and parental 'chauvinism' by about one-quarter (7 per cent significant, 19 per cent minor). It is interesting to note that, despite parallels drawn with the experience of American schools' involvement with parents, relatively few schools (7 per cent) report problems with parents who try to take over the class or the school, and that fewer still (3 per cent) consider it a significant problem. In fact this is the last frequently encountered problem of all, and is not related to school type.

Just under one-third of primary schools consider a lack of confidentiality on the part of some parents, in respect of what they discover in school, to be a problem (7 per cent significant, 25 per cent minor). However, neither complaints from parents who are not involved about those who are, or parents wishing to help in school 'for the wrong reasons' are seen as major problems.

Staff unwillingness to allow parents into their classrooms is seen as a problem by about one-quarter of primary schools (8 per cent significant, 15 per cent minor), and parental lack of understanding about the aims of the school and criticism of what teachers do, by about one-fifth (3 per cent significant, 15 per cent minor). This issue is taken up in greater depth in Chapter 7.

Other problems (5 per cent) reported by head-teachers include: lack of confidence in themselves on the part of parents; toddlers accompanying parents; a lack of space to accommodate parents wishing to help, and hostility on the part of paid ancillary staff, anxious about the security of their employment.

General Aspects

Only 12 per cent of all primary schools provide after-school care facilities for children though another 33 per cent run after-school clubs or activities which serve this general purpose. Both these forms of provision are significantly related to school type, the practice being much more prevalent in schools catering for the older age-range.

Nine per cent of schools have a room set aside for use by parents or other members of the community and 37 per cent have facilities open for the use of their local communities after school hours. Again, these facilities are significantly related to school type; the former being more often found in schools for younger children, and the latter, older children.

Two of the case study schools had 'Parents' Rooms'. At Tyler primary, funds had been made available under the Community Education Project, of which the school was part, to renovate and equip a room at the top of the old school building for parents' use. The room was brightly decorated and provided with easy chairs, low tables and facilities for making tea. It was in regular use by parents for committee meetings or just a 'cuppa and a gossip'.

The deputy-head of Mill Street nursery explained the uses made of the Parents Room at her school:

> Well, it started off by being a meeting room. We didn't really have anywhere that the parents could go and it's useful when parents are settling children so that they just don't have to go wandering round for 10 minutes or go home if they are leaving their child just for a short time at the beginning. It might only be 10 minutes at first and if they live a long way away, it's a bit like killing time, so it's nice if they've got a room they can come and sit in. The

child thinks they've gone shopping or something, and doesn't know they are still within the school. So they've got somewhere where they can come and sit and in that way they very often meet other mothers; in an area like this you find there's quite a lot of mothers who don't go out to work and who are really quite lonely. We've also had various people in to give talks to the mothers; we've had people from the Social Services and people talking about how they could get better help from their doctor, which is all very helpful to the mother. We also have special classes; for instance we have a class for Asian ladies who want to learn English, which is helpful for them, and we've also got a home liaison worker, though she's not called that. She comes in three mornings a week and if any parents have any problems they can take them to her.

Over one-half (58 per cent) of all primary schools publish newletters informing parents about general school activities. this practice is significantly related to school type, increasing in prevalence with the ages of children involved. That relatively fewer (24 per cent) nurseries do so is probably due to the immediate, day-to-day nature of their contact with parents, enabling them to pass on news by word of mouth rather than needing to resort to a written newsletter. Newsletters were generally sent out (by 31 per cent of all schools) once or twice a term.

About half of all primary schools send written reports concerning children's work and/or behaviour to parents. They are most often sent once a year (39 per cent), more rarely (7 per cent) twice a year. This practice is very much more common in schools for older primary children (junior and middle) and hardly occurs at all (1 per cent) in nursery schools.

Home visits by head-teachers or members of the teaching staff are carried out in one-fifth of primary schools as a matter of school policy and more frequently in nurseries and schools with nursery classes. In addition, for almost one-half of primary schools, home visiting is carried out by another person attached to the school.

Home visits were made by the nursery teacher at Tyler primary to all prospective parents to establish contact and a friendly relationship. At Carford primary this task was carried out by a specially designated 'compensatory' teacher, Mrs Knowles. She described this part of her job:

I'm supposed to do home visits before the children come into school and follow-up visits after they've been there a short while. I go beforehand to ask the parents if there's anything they want to know about the school, anything they want to tell me about the child and also to get a view of the child. You can see what sort of things they're doing, how they react, and make a very brief note about anything that might give the class teacher a clue as to what to expect; nothing too deep because I don't think it's fair; they can give a totally incorrect impression sometimes; they may act differently at home to how they act at school.

The head of Elm Road infants, however, didn't believe in home visiting by teachers and explained why:

I don't personally advocate home visiting myself because I think it would be just too overwhelming. I think the problems are too great; we have far too many and I don't think to get too emotionally involved would really help. You've got to have limitations, you can only do things for children and parents within the school and try to liaise with other agencies outside.

The head of Riverside nursery also had misgivings about making home visits, but for different reasons:

I believe the relationship between the members of a family is very important and only if we are invited should teachers enter into this domain. If I go into someone's home, I cannot speak freely in the way that I could if that person came to me at school where I am at home, if I can put it like that. I have in fact tried going into the home for this purpose but have found that I am distracted, either by the atmosphere there or, by other members of the family. At home the mother may talk about a whole range of problems or difficulties which although interesting are not necessarily about the child. When a mother comes to the nursery where she has brought her child, the child is the centre of her attention and mine and we can more easily discuss problems relating to that child in the educational setting.

Ninety-six per cent of primary schools have a Board of Managers and 67 per cent of these include elected or coopted parents, though they generally constitute less than one-fifth of the total Board.

Parents are very rarely involved in decisions concerning the curriculum (4 per cent), with the notable exception of sex education (43 per cent), demonstrating the unique nature of perceptions about this pastoral aspect of the curriculum. The consultation of parents over sex education is significantly related to school type, hardly ever occurring in nursery schools!

Aims and Attitudes

Over one-half (59 per cent) of primary head-teachers would like to see a greater number of parents involved in school activities and 52 per cent would like to see parents involved in a wider variety of activities. One-fifth consider that they already have so much parental involvement that it would not be practical to extend in any further.

Fifty-five per cent of primary heads believe that parental involvement has increased over the past two years and 63 per cent of heads believe that parental attitudes have changed markedly as a result. Perceived changes in specific parental attitudes are shown in Table 3.4. Only one of these items, 'parents derive personal benefit from their involvement with school activities', was significantly related to school type, being more commonly found in schools catering for the lower age-range.

Finally, the principal educational roles attributed to parents in head's written-in comments include: support for their children in school, a demonstration of interest in their school achievements and problems, cooperation with teaching staff to consolidate agreed policies for children's welfare and help in widening children's horizons and social contact.

This chapter has been devoted to considering the relationship between parental involvement and school type. It must be admitted at

Table 3.4: **Changes in parental attitudes**

	All Primary Schools, %
Parents find it easier to visit the school to talk to teachers or head	61
Parents and teachers understand each other more easily	59
Parents have a greater appreciation of the difficulties with which teachers have to contend	58
Parents have a greater appreciation of the school's educational objectives	54
Parents derive personal benefit from their involvement with school activities	50
Parents take a greater interest in their children's education	48
Parents give greater support to school functions, open days, etc.	47
Parents have a deeper understanding of modern educational methods in use in their children's school	38

this stage that there is little evidence to support the hypothesis that the presence of a nursery unit in a school increases the likelihood of a higher level of parental involvement. There is, however, some evidence that classroom based involvement is generally greater and more frequently reported in schools catering for the lower age-range. The relative infrequency of formal contacts, such as newsletters and school reports in nursery and infant schools, suggests that daily informal contact renders these unnecessary.

Chapter 4

Types of Parental Involvement

In the last chapter, parental involvement was reported and discussed taking each aspect in turn. Where differences in involvement at the various stages of primary education (as represented by the six types of school) reached statistical significance, these were reported and their implications considered. The disadvantage with this piecemeal approach is that, whilst it adequately depicts the different aspects of parental involvement in primary schools in general, it does not show how they *fit together* in any particular type of school.

In order to establish whether there were distinctive *types* of parental involvement, and if so, whether they were related to the age of the children, those questionnaire items which deal with aspects of parental involvement were listed and cluster analysed. In all, 53 items in the questionnaire which sought information about specific aspects of parental involvement were suitable for this purpose by reason of their 'independence' of other items and were included. For convenience they are listed in Appendix (iii), Table 1.

Cluster analysis is a process by which the schools (in this instance) were grouped together according to similarities in their responses to the 53 questionnaire items. The process starts with the pairing of the most similar schools, and progresses by the gradual building up of larger groups by the attachment of other schools to each initial pairing in such a way as to keep the within-groups differences to a minimum. As the process proceeds, whole groups merge with one another (accompanied by an increase in the within-groups differences) and finally all schools merge into one crude cluster. The two extremes are thus represented at the outset by all schools being considered unique and at the finish by them all being crudely the same. The value of the technique lies at some point intermediate between these extremes where most of the schools are members of one group or another but the within-groups differences are still reasonably small. The interpretation of the results of cluster analysis is therefore to some extent a matter of judgement.

There were over 1,400 schools about which survey information had been collected, far more than the computer could handle.[1] It was therefore necessary to sample amongst these for clustering. Two random samples of 250 were drawn and cluster-analysed. The clusters which emerged in each case were closely similar in composition, and this was accepted as evidence that the clustering probably applied equally well to the rest.

There was a tendency for schools of a similar type, as defined by the sampling frame for the survey, to cluster together (i.e. nursery schools with other nursery schools, infants' schools with other infants' schools, etc.). However, the 'best' level of association seemed to be one where two main clusters coalesced, the one mainly of schools for children of infant and nursery age, the other of schools for children of junior age.

There are clear reasons for accepting such a dichotomy. For instance, children of infant age and below are generally accompanied to and from school by parents, which automatically facilitates a casual regular contact with the school. As children reach the junior years, parents accompany them to school less frequently (Sadler, 1972). There is, however, no need to speculate as to what characterizes this dichotomy, since the means exist for exploring it in detail in relation to the 53 characteristics of parent–school involvement used to produce it.

In order to map out the way in which the features distinguish between parental involvement of the type characteristic of the two clusters, the data on the 53 features in respect of all the schools in the survey were submitted to discriminant analysis. This is a statistical process first developed for botanical classification. It produces a function which is the combination of features which best distinguishes between two or more groups or families. For plants the 'features' are

---

[1] The larger the number of features of each school, the more computer capacity is required by this technique. In practice this means that the number of schools which can be clustered at one time is directly proportional to the number of features which are used in the process of comparison and allocation to groups. With 53 features the number was limited to about 250.

number and shape of leaves, petals, stamens, etc. As used in this present connection, the features were the 53 questionnaire items listed in Appendix (iii), Table 1.

Of these 51 made a statistically significant contribution to discriminating between the two types of schools. The function formed out of the combination of these 51 questionnaire items correctly classified just over 90 per cent of the schools in the survey, 96 per cent of schools for nursery and infant children, and 88 per cent of schools for junior children. There was thus a greater homogeneity in parental involvement amongst the schools for the younger children than there was amongst the schools for the older children. The probable reason for this is the inclusion in the 'older' cluster of JMI or combined primary schools a few of which also had nursery units which therefore tended to manifest some of the features of schools for the younger children. This can be seen as further circumstantial evidence for the effect of the ages of the children on the type of parental involvement.

In considering the ways in which the features characterize the kind of parental involvement in the two types of schools, it must be realized that the differences are not total and absolute, but are rather of emphasis.

At the beginning of Chapter 3 it was hypothesized that nursery schools and schools with nursery classes would involve parents to a greater degree than other schools catering for children of primary school age. Limited support for this hypothesis was found in the data, classroom based involvement being more frequently reported in schools catering for the lower age-range. This distinction, between schools catering for the upper and lower age-ranges, is now borne out by the results of the cluster analysis. Thus the most important characteristic[1] of the schools for younger children is the casual day-to-day contact with parents made possible by them bringing their children to school in the morning and collecting them in the afternoon. In contrast the most important characteristic of schools for older children is parents' provision of transport for children for 'away' football or other school team games. These two features provide an unsurprising contrast between the types of parental involvement mainly associated with each group: team games do not generally occur at infant and nursery level, and by the time children reach the junior age-range, they are usually allowed to come to school unaccompanied. Of more interest, perhaps,

---

[1] The rank order of importance of features as discriminators is given in Appendix (iii), Tables 2 and 3.

are the remaining features characterizing each group. Thus schools for younger children emphasize both the sending of written information to 'new' parents and the invitation to these parents to visit the school before their children start. Once the children have actually begun attending, however, it is schools for the older children which emphasize the invitation of parents to open days or evenings, and make provision for them to discuss their children's work with the head or class teacher *by appointment*. The two types also differ in the manner in which they explain the curriculum to parents. Schools for younger children feature the explanation of teaching methods *in advance* to 'new' parents while schools for older children feature the on-going invitation of parents to workshop meetings to discuss their children's work.

Apart from parents helping generally in the classroom, which is characteristic of schools for younger children, all aspects of school-based parental involvement (Question 10e) — parents' help on schools' visits and outings, parents' sewing (costumes for plays, etc.), parents with specialist knowledge giving talks, helping to dress children after swimming, hearing children read, helping with football, running library schemes, doing major repairs in the school, helping with craft-work, helping in the school library — characterize schools for older children, in that order of importance.

Question 11 was concerned with what the school offered parents (other than an education for their child). The explicit provision of after-school care for children and its more indirect counterpart, after-school clubs serving the same purpose both characterize schools for older children. The provision of a room or other accommodation *set aside* for use by parents and the community generally is characteristic of schools for younger children. The provision of 'school facilities' outside of the school hours for the use of the community is the weakest of all discriminators between schools for younger and older children. Next to it in rank order is the publication of a school newsletter, which is a weak characteristic of schools for older children. In contrast, the sending of school reports to parents is the second strongest characteristic of schools for older children. The 'bussing' of children, and home visiting by the head or teachers as a matter of policy are both characteristic of schools for older children, whereas home visiting by 'other agencies', such as home–school liaison officer characterizes schools for younger children, but only weakly so. The existence of a managing body is characteristic of schools for older children but the presence of a parent as a coopted member of such managing body characterizes schools for younger children.

The comparative success with which the clusters are 'statistically separated' lends substantial support to viewing the type of parental involvement as being considerably affected by the age of the children concerned. Of the 53 features, only two were set aside from the analysis as making no significant contribution to discrimination.

Chapter 5

Factors Influencing School-Based Parental Involvement

The project brief specified that an attempt be made to indicate the factors which influence the level of school-based parental involvement, as determined by answers to Question 10e (38–51). What some of these might be was tentatively suggested at the outset, and the first of these factors, pupil age (as represented by the different categories of primary school), has already been dealt with in Chapter 3. The design (architecture) of the school building, the organization of the curriculum, and the size of the school (pupils on roll) were also expected to be of importance. Above all, from the literature, it was expected that parents' social class would be a crucial variable, and this view was endorsed in every school visited during the period of questionnaire development.

In addition to these factors, various others were suggested during school visits, and those frequently cited were included in the final form of the questionnaire as Questions 1–8 inclusive.

Table 5.1: Factors external to the school

Social class of parents	Q6a, 8a, 8d
Ethnic origins of pupils	Q8c
Working mothers	Q8e
Pupil turnover	Q8f
Changes in the size of school roll	Q7a
Connection with a church	Q6b

The factors may be subdivided into two main types: factors external to the schools and factors internal to the schools, and will be discussed in that sequence.

Social Class of Parents

> Variations in what children learn in school depend largely on variations in what they bring to school, not on variations in what schools offer them. (Jencks, 1975.)

Studies of educational achievement emphasize the importance of the child's social background and the crucial role played by parents in fostering in their children positive attitudes towards schools (Peaker, 1971).

Social class-related disparity in achievement is manifested particularly in post-compulsory schooling when children from Classes Four and Five on the Registrar General's Scale are under-represented in establishments of higher education (GB, Ministry of Education, 1959).

School location (Question 6) and background information (Question 8) were designed to elicit information on the general social and economic circumstances of a school's parents and children. The information was obtained, as for the rest of the questionnaire, from head-teachers and the case study material supports the view that they are reliable informants regarding the general characteristics of parents, children and catchment areas. The information on the parents' social environment nevertheless remains as the head-teachers' broad characterizations and, in the absence of direct data from parents, it was not possible to construct a measure of social class which would take into account the composite nature of that variable. For the purposes of this project three questionnaire items were deemed suitable as indicators of social class. These are Question 6a:37 on housing categories and school location, Question 8a:43 on type of parental employment and Question 8d:50 on the percentage of children receiving free school meals. This last has the merit of being the most objective of the measures available since head teachers would be in a position to provide accurate information. Wedge and Prosser (1973) used this in *Born to Fail* as a measure of poverty. Its main disadvantage lies in lack of take-up on the part of those entitled to free school meals but it seems adequate as a crude measure of low income and the social deprivation with which it is normally associated.

These items were cross-tabulated with each other for primary schools in aggregate (as for all analyses of data reported in this chapter), the data being weighted to reflect the correct population proportions of the six school types. The analysis confirmed the expected relationships between these three items, all of them being significant beyond the 0.001 level. Thus parents of children in 81 per cent of schools in areas of poor housing are characterized as having non-professional or unskilled jobs; while parents of children in 64 per cent of schools in suburban areas dominated by private housing are largely in professional or managerial occupations (see Appendix (iv), Table 1).

Similarly, in 50 per cent of schools situated in poor housing areas (Location 1), over a quarter of the children are receiving free school meals and the same is the case for 60 per cent and 43 per cent of schools in Locations 2 and 3 respectively (see Appendix (iv), Table 2). It is of interest to note, in view of the lack of take-up mentioned earlier, that in 15 per cent of all primary schools, over a quarter of the children are in receipt of free school meals. Although take-up of this benefit is believed to be high when compared to take-up of other benefits, a recent estimate, by the Child Poverty Action Group (Bradshawe and Weale, 1978) based on official figures, suggests that 460,000 poor children are not receiving the free school dinner to which they would be entitled.

The incidence of children receiving free school meals is markedly lower where their parents are characterized as largely in professional or managerial positions, whereas 42 per cent of schools where the children's parents are unskilled or non-professional workers have over a quarter of their children receiving free school meals (see Appendix (iv), Table 3).

While no claims are made that these three items serve as a *complete* measure of the composite social class variable, the degree to which they interrelate suggests that they represent it adequately. The cross-tabulation of the three items shows that the strongest association occurs between parents' occupation and the area in which they live; the weakest occurs between the school's area and the number of its children receiving free school meals. Since there is little to indicate which single item is superior, each one was separately cross-tabulated with school-based parental involvement (Question 10e: 38–51).

The relationship between school-based parental involvement and school location proved the least clear of the three. Although there is a statistically significant relationship between the prevalence of involvement in seven of the activities specified under Question 10e and school location the only clear trend is towards peaks of involvement in schools serving urban or suburban areas with smaller, privately-owned houses and suburban areas with larger, privately-owned houses (see Appendix (iv), Table 4). In addition it appears that schools serving rural or semi-rural areas have a generally lower level of involvement of parents, except for the provision of transport for away football matches. This type of activity can be regarded as involving a different kind of effort on the part of parents than would be the case in activities where they help regularly in the classroom. Provision of transport is a necessity in rather isolated areas, and is of a spasmodic nature, not requiring regular attendance in schools.

The relationship between the levels of school based involvement and free school meals provision is significant for four types of involvement. The relationship is less pervasive than that with school location, but rather clearer, with a definite trend towards lower levels of involvement being generally apparent as the level of free school meal provision rises (see Appendix (iv), Table 5).

When parental involvement was analysed by the head-teachers' general classification of parents' employment status, associations with 10 types were indicated (see Appendix (iv), Table 6). Higher levels of involvement in all activities consistently occur in schools whose parents work in managerial or professional capacities as compared with schools where parents are characterized as either largely unskilled or skilled and semi-skilled. This is consistent with previous findings (see Chapter 1) that working-class parents appear to be less involved with their children's education than are middle-class parents. Lower levels of involvement do not necessarily imply less *interest* on the part of parents. Clearly, economic and social factors influence the ability of parents to help in schools. For instance, the wide differences in the percentages of parents helping with transport may be partly a function of the availability of a car and being able to afford petrol. Similarly, if an assumption is made that parents working in unskilled or skilled and semi-skilled capacities also have a generally lower level of educational attainment than professional or managerial parents, it could tentatively be suggested that it is the latter who will be more frequently asked and more able to cope with activities which require literacy, e.g. hearing children read. Several teachers in one of the case study schools, designated as an educational priority school, commented adversely on the competence of the school's parents, many of whom were illiterate.

Though they tried to accommodate as many as offered their help, they admitted that it was difficult to find suitable activities for some.

Where activities require parents' help at a practical level a relatively higher level of involvement occurs in schools with parents in a working-class occupation. Even so, only 74 per cent of schools with such parents have help on school trips compared with 89 per cent of schools where parents are in professional or managerial occupations. Fifty-seven per cent of schools with unskilled parents and 64 per cent of schools with skilled and semi-skilled parents receive help with needlework compared with 72 per cent of schools with parents in managerial or professional occupations.

Two parents from one of the case study schools in a deprived area explained why they had not gone into school to help, in spite of having ample time in which to do so:

> I like cooking but I do it my own way. I couldn't use the proper measures like they would want at school.

> They never seem to want help; they've never asked me anyway. I would have helped if they had ... They never send a letter asking what parents would like to do in the school and I don't feel I could just walk in and out without a purpose or an invitation telling me what time to go.

The difficulties encountered by parents in offering their help to their children's school are discussed more fully in Chapter 8.

To sum up, it would seem that membership of a particular social class exerts a definite influence on the likelihood of parents helping in their children's school. The more 'professional' the parents' occupation, the more well-off they are, the better the area in which they live, then the more likely they are to become actively involved in their children's schooling. What cannot be determined, of course, is whether the relative lack of involvement among working-class parents can be attributed to these parents' lack of interest, to the school's unwillingness to involve them, or perhaps to some other factor as yet untested. Of the three measures of the social class of parents, school location seems to show the strongest associations with other factors influencing parental involvement (Appendix (iv), Table 22), in particular with school size; school architecture; staff—pupil ratio, and pupils' ethnic origins. This pattern of association is not generally followed by either of the other measures of social class. It is, however, a fact that parental involvement seems to add yet another string to the bow of middle-class educational advantage.

Ethnic Origins of Pupils

A group of pupils commonly held to be disadvantaged are those of non-British ethnic origin. It has been suggested (Hegarty and Lucas, 1978), for instance, that they are more frequently ascertained educationally subnormal than is warranted by the normal distribution of abilities, and that cultural incompatabilities with the majority population, and particularly (but not solely) in the case of those of Asian origin, linguistic difficulties are possible explanations for this. It is logical to expect that these cultural and linguistic incompatabilities will also affect the involvement of the parents in school and classroom based activities. This expectation is barely borne out by the data (Appendix (iv), Tables 7, a, b, c). Only one type of parental involvement — help with transport to away games — is consistently, and inversely, associated with the prevalence of pupils of non-British ethnic origin, at a level reaching statistical significance.

The data also suggest, less consistently (pupils of Asian origin only, Table 7b), that the incidence of parents helping to dress children after PE, similarly declines. The former may well be accounted for, in part at any rate, by the association between pupils' ethnic origins and the measures of social class (Appendix (iv), Table 22). Closer inspection of the relationship between this factor and school location reveals a marked (and not unexpected) tendency for schools with higher levels of such children to be concentrated in Locations 1 and 2 ('Houses are packed together in a poor state of repair', and 'An area of council housing characterized by high-rise flats'). In these schools the need for such transport may be less by reason of the relatively closer proximity of the other schools where away games occur. The data also reveal that schools with many pupils of non-British ethnic origin are also characterized by a high incidence of free school meals (indicative of communal poverty), and a preponderance of parents in non-professional occupations. It will be recalled that these factors are associated with low levels of school and classroom based parental involvement (Tables 5 and 6). The decline in help with dressing children after PE and swimming when associated with increases in the numbers of pupils of Asian ethnic origin may be related to cultural background. Alternatively, it is possible that swimming facilities are less often available to these schools, and that they are less strict about children changing their clothes for PE. However, this association may quite possibly be a function of some confounding variable as yet contested.

Working Mothers

The problems of 'working mothers' and of their families have been well rehearsed over the years. It is axiomatic that mothers who have regular jobs cannot at the same time be available to help in the classroom or generally in the school during school hours. They are not, of course, precluded from helping outside school hours, though it was commonly suggested during the development of the questionnaire that they are less likely to have the time and energy to spare than mothers who are not working. It was, therefore, expected that there would be an inverse relationship between all school and classroom based forms of parental involvement and the proportion of children in a school with working mothers.

There is only one type of parental involvement — hearing children read — which is significantly associated with the number of working mothers, and this shows a clear tendency to *increase* as the proportion of children with working mothers rises. It is difficult to suggest plausible explanations for this finding, which appears to conflict with common-sense. The proportion of working mothers is significantly (but only slightly) associated with most of the other factors influencing parental involvement (Table 22), most notably school size, pupils' ethnic origins, and the social class variables. However, 'parents hearing children read' is only significantly associated with school size (increasing with increase in school size, Table 16) and type of parental employment (occurring more frequently in schools characterized by parents in professional or management occupations, Table 6). The data show that children in large schools are much more likely to have mothers who work than those in small schools, but schools where parents are mostly in professional or managerial occupations have fewer children with working mothers. This interrelationship between the proportion of children with working mothers and school size may well account for this improbable finding. The interrelationship with the social class finding does not.

An alternative explanation suggests itself: that head teachers subscribing to popular beliefs about the deprivation suffered by the children of working mothers, are concerned to increase the reading experience and the personal contact with an adult that accompanies hearing children read. Furthermore, where the majority of mothers are out at work, there may be a relatively weak community of 'at home' mothers to provide mutual social support, and this may turn the attentions of non-working mothers toward the school as an alternative.

Pupil Turnover

Population mobility has been a marked characteristic of the post-war years. Recently it was estimated (Hodges, 1977) that 625,000 children move house every year and for many of these children, and by extension, their parents, this implies a change of school also. It is commonly held that such mobility, inevitably accompanied by a break in continuity, is detrimental to children's education, although this assumption has recently been queried (Lacey and Blane, 1979). Whatever the direct effect on children's education, a too frequent need to make new relationships, both in the neighbourhood generally and in the school particularly, has been cited (Fried, 1963) as resulting in families becoming more self-sufficient and 'withdrawn', hence less likely to be involved in the life of the school.

Data on the association between school and classroom based involvement and pupil turnover were derived from Questions 8f:52, 53. For four of the 13 aspects there is a statistically significant relationship (Appendix (iv), Table 9). For three aspects – help on school visits and outings, help with craft work, cooking, music, etc., and hearing children read – the relationships with pupil turnover are curvilinear, that is they tend to increase up to a point beyond which they decrease. A school may welcome 'new blood' and for their part, the geographically (and in many cases socially) mobile are willing and able to become involved in the lives of schools whose communities they briefly join. Beyond a certain point, however, the turnover becomes too rapid and the difficulties associated with involving parents in these relatively intimate aspects of school life outweigh the perceived benefits. Help with the fourth type of involvement with which pupil turnover is significantly associated – transport to away games – declines steadily as the rate of pupil turnover increases. This is probably a consequence of schools being progressively less able to rely on the regular availability of such help and having to make alternative arrangements.

Pupil turnover is relatively independent of the other factors influencing parental involvement (Appendix (iv), Table 22).

Changes in the Size of School Roll

The number of children on roll in a school is determined mainly by the general level of fertility in the community it serves and by the pattern of new building in its catchment area. For many years following the Second World War there was a general tendency for the number of children on roll in most primary schools to rise steadily as new houses were built in the vicinity. Sometimes numbers increased dramatically when large-scale building development occurred, but this was generally followed a little while later by the building of a new school. Fluctuation in the size of a school's roll is thus normal. However, recent changes in the lifestyle of young people, coupled with the advent of more reliable and widely available methods of contraception, have led to a sharp reduction[1] in the number of children passing through the education system and this general decline is, of course, affecting primary schools first.

Data derived from the present survey suggests that in 1977, rolls were rising in 15 per cent of schools, falling in 28 per cent and static in the rest (Question 7a:39). School and classroom based parental involvement tends to increase where rolls are rising and vice versa. This relationship only reaches statistical significance for one type of involvement: 'parents with specialist knowledge, e.g. local policemen, fireman, etc., give talks to children' (Appendix (iv), Table 10).

Change in school roll is interrelated with several of the other factors influencing parental involvement, notably school location (Table 4) and staff turnover (Table 21). However, help from parents with specialist knowledge only reaches statistical significance for school location, where it tends to be more commonly associated with the more 'middle-class' locations. The data show rising school rolls also to be more commonly associated with such locations (Question 37:4, 5 and 6). Help from parents with specialist knowledge may thus partly be a by-product of the type of location in which school rolls are rising, as well as being a natural outcome of the increasing pool of parental expertise potentially available to such schools.

Connection with a Church

Finally in this section, the influence on a school of a formal link with a Roman Catholic or Church of England parish will be considered (Question 6b:38). Family membership of a church and the attendance of children at the associated church school was frequently cited by head-teachers as a significant influence on parental involvement in the life of the school. For three aspects of school and classroom-based involvement, there is a significant association with being a church school (Appendix (iv), Table 11). But for each of these the relationship is

---

[1] Figures as high as 40 per cent reduction over the period mid-1970s to mid-1980s are currently being forecast.

negative: parents being less likely to help with craft work, cooking, generally in the classroom and with specialist talks.

It seems probable that other aspects of church schools, located in the schools themselves rather than their communities, are confounding the (expected positive) effects of a 'religious connection'. It is the experience of the project team that in general, church schools tend to be more 'traditional' in their curriculum organization than non-church schools. The data reveal a modest (but statistically significant) relationship between church schools and curriculum organization and school architecture: that church schools are predominantly organized in a traditional manner (Question 5:35, 36, category 3, with basic subjects in the morning and 'creative' activities in the afternoon, and category 6, class teaching with a structured curriculum); and that they are usually of traditional design (Question 4:32, 33, categories 1, 2 and 3) characterized by 'box-classrooms' with little space for activities which might involve parents during the school day. These school features are all negatively associated with the various in-school and in-class forms of parental involvement (Tables 12, 13, 14 and 15).

Table 5.2: Factors internal to the school

School architecture	Q4
Curriculum organization	Q5
School size (No. on roll)	Q2a
Pupil—teacher ratio	Q2b
Level of in-school behaviour problems	Q8g
Staff turnover	Q7b
Period of head's incumbency	Q7c

School Architecture and Curriculum Organization

At the outset it had been expected that the level of school and classroom based parental involvement would be directly related both to the 'architectural openness' of a school, and to the informality of its teaching approach. Since these are strongly interrelated (Appendix (iv), Table 22), it is proposed to discuss them together rather than separately.

The experience of the project team during visits made to a variety of schools suggested that it is easier for any 'outsiders', whether researchers or parents, to gain access to a school with open teaching areas which they may enter without attracting undue attention.

A closed classroom door, on the other hand, may be more than enough to deter parents who possibly remember their own school days with decidedly mixed feelings. It also seemed that teachers working in a cooperative or team-teaching situation appeared far more at ease working with, and being watched by, other adults than those teaching alone.

It was decided that each age-group, i.e. nursery, infant and junior, should be treated separately for the purpose of this analysis. For the *nursery* age-group there is no significant relationship between level of school-based parental involvement and either school architecture or organization. This may possibly be accounted for by the relatively undifferentiated architecture and curriculum of most nursery schools and classes.

The relationship between level of parental involvement and school architecture for the infant age-group is statistically significant for five types and between parental involvement and curriculum organization also for five types (see Appendix (iv), Tables 12 and 13). As might be expected, these activities are almost exclusively those which are classroom-based, including parents hearing children read, helping with craft work, and helping generally in the classroom. Levels of parental involvement appear to be appreciably higher in infant schools with more 'open' architecture and employing an integrated-day teaching approach.

The relationship between school and classroom based parental involvement and school architecture and organization for the *junior* age range appears to be somewhat more tenuous. Thus there is a statistically significant association between school architecture and four types of parental involvement (see Appendix (iv), Table 14), and between curriculum organization and three types of parental involvement (Table 15). As for infant schools, the classroom based types of involvement predominate, and occur more frequently in schools with more 'open' architecture, and in schools organizing the curriculum on an 'integrated' rather than a traditional, 'collected' basis. Integration, in fact, appears to be a more important influence on parental involvement than either vertical versus horizontal grouping, or team versus individual teaching. This coincides with expectation: it is likely to be more desirable, and much easier, to make use of the extra help afforded by the presence of a parent in a classroom where a variety of activities involving relatively small groups of children are taking place, than where the whole class is involved in one activity under the direct control of the teacher.

School Size

School size had been suggested as an influence on levels of parental involvement by several of the head teachers contacted during the development of the questionnaire. For the purpose of this analysis, nursery, infants and juniors were considered together, with the size of the school being defined in Question 2a of the questionnaire by the number of pupils on roll. Part-time pupils were counted as full-time to avoid confusion, especially in nursery classes and schools.

The grouping of schools by size corresponds with those used by the Burnham Committee on teachers' salaries; thus Group 1 schools have less than 50 children, Group 2, 51 to 100 children and so on. There is a general trend towards higher levels of involvement in larger schools, reaching statistical significance in respect of five types (Appendix (iv), Table 16). There is one notable exception to this trend: help with transport to away games, etc., occurs nearly as often in the two smallest categories of school as it does in the two largest. This may be due to the smaller schools frequently being located in rural or semi-rural areas where the need for transport facilities provided by parents is consequently greater. By the same token it is less easy for parents to make regular attendances at such schools for classroom activities.

School size is significantly associated with most of the other factors influencing school and classroom based parental involvement, notably with staff–pupil ratios, school architecture and school location. The smaller schools tend to have more favourable staff–pupil ratios, and to be of more traditional design. The larger schools tend to be in Locations 3 and 4 (Question 6a:37), large council and private housing estates respectively. School and classroom based parental involvement is significantly associated with all these factors (Tables 17 and 18, 12 and 14, 4) in ways generally consistent with its association with school size, suggesting that the influence of each is to some extent a by-product of its relationship with the others.

Staff–Pupil Ratio

Staff–pupil ratio had also been suggested by head-teachers as influential in determining levels of school and classroom based parental involvement. As with school architecture and curriculum organization, the data were analysed separately for the nursery, infant and junior age ranges.

Staff–pupil ratio is not significantly associated with parental involvement for the *nursery* age range. For the *infant* age range it is associated with five types (Appendix (iv), Table 17), increasing as pupil–teacher ratios become less favourable. This effect is more pronounced for *junior* schools, where there is a statistically significant relationship with seven types of school and classroom based parental involvement (Appendix (iv), Table 18), again increasing as the pupil–teacher ratio becomes less favourable. It is tempting to conclude that where staff–pupil ratios are less favourable, parents are to some extent substituting for teaching and ancillary staff. Alternatively, since staff–pupil ratio is significantly associated with school architecture, curriculum organization, and school size it is probable that much of its apparent influence is explained by their influence (see the discussion in the previous section and at the end of this chapter, p. 71).

Level of In-school Behaviour Problems

In-school behaviour problems, the origins of which are often thought to lie in children's home or family circumstances, were also cited by several head-teachers during the development of the questionnaire as influencing levels of parental involvement. It was suggested that for such children the presence of their parent(s) in school might well make matters worse and for that reason school and classroom-based involvement would be less prevalent where such problems were seen to exist.

Three-quarters of primary school head-teachers consider that their pupils' in-school behaviour problems are related to home or family circumstances. This belief is, however, associated with *higher* levels of parental involvement than is the case for schools where home and family circumstances are not thought to be related to in-school behaviour problems. For three types of involvement, classroom as well as school-based, the association reaches statistical significance (Appendix (iv), Table 19).

A possible inference is that heads who are conscious of the possible effects of children's home background show greater awareness of children with problems attributable to home circumstances and are thus more willing to promote home–school relationships.

This factor is significantly but only slightly interrelated with most of the others. Its strongest association appears to be with pupils' ethnic origins, school location, and head's incumbency, but it tends on the whole to influence different types of involvement from these factors, and may therefore be considered to exert a more or less independent influence.

Staff Turnover and Period of Head-teacher's Incumbency

The last two factors to be considered in this section relate to the teachers and the heads themselves. They are moderately interrelated (Table 22) and are both indicative of stability in staffing, and will therefore be discussed together.

The years from 1945 until the early 1970s were characterized by a chronic and seemingly permanent overall shortage of teachers. It has been argued that this, combined with the system of teacher salary differentials, led to high levels of staff turnover with a weakening of continuity in relationships between schools and their communities as the direct (and undesirable) consequence. The enlarged teacher training programme, combined with a sharp fall in the birthrate over the past decade, and recent reductions in public expenditure, have had a dramatic effect on the employment prospects of teachers, and turnover (of both heads and assistants) has sharply declined. In 1973 teacher turnover was running at an average level of 20 per cent per annum, and at an average of 25 per cent in certain inner-city areas (Great Britain, 1977, para. 3:1, p. 16). Data from the present survey suggest that in over half of primary schools the turnover of assistants averaged less than 10 per cent per annum over the previous two years (i.e. 1975–77), and that in almost two-thirds of primary schools, heads have been in their present posts for more than five years.

The relationship between school and classroom based parental involvement is slightly stronger with the period of head-teachers' present incumbency than with teacher turnover. There is a statistically significant association between five types of involvement and heads' incumbency (Appendix (iv), Table 20) and four types of involvement and staff turnover (Appendix (iv), Table 21).

Interestingly, the influence of these complementary indicators of school stability on parental involvement shows a tendency to be curvilinear, particularly in the case of heads' incumbency. Parental involvement increases as staff stability decreases, then, beyond a certain point, declines again. In all cases, school and classroom based parental involvement is least frequent in the most 'stable' schools, as indicated by the period of the present head's incumbency, and, in all but one, as indicated by staff turnover. This sole exception is when parents help generally in the classroom, a form of involvement particularly vulnerable to changeover of teachers.

During the period of questionnaire development, it was frequently suggested by heads that it was not until they had been 'in office' for

some time ('several years' was often quoted) that they had felt sufficiently confident deliberately to involve parents intimately in the life of
their school. The data suggest that this is true generally for primary
school heads. The decline in such involvement beyond a certain point
in a head-teacher's term of office is less easy to explain. There are two
possibilities: first, there may be progressive disenchantment with the
rewards gained for the effort required to involve parents in the life of
the school; secondly, parental involvement having only recently become
at all widespread, some of the longer serving head-teachers might be
exercising caution before setting out on what they view as uncharted
waters. Whatever the reason, the relative lack of statistically significant
associations with other factors influencing parental involvement (Table
22) suggests the very considerable *de jure* power of the primary school
head, in this as in other aspects of school life.

Caution or disenchantment on the one hand, and too little continuity of relationships on the other may similarly account for the
curvilinear association between parental involvement and staff turnover.
Reference to Table 22 (Appendix (iv)) shows that, like heads' incumbency it is only weakly interrelated with other factors influencing
parental involvement. There is also a moderate association with changes
in school roll, in respect of which it mainly influences different types
of involvement, thus further underlining its independence as a factor.

Interrelationships between Factors

Throughout the discussion in this chapter of the influence of the
various factors on school and classroom-based parental involvement,
constant reference has been made to the interrelationships *amongst*
them. Whilst each undoubtedly exerts a unique influence on involvement, because of the interrelationships (set out in matrix form in Table
22, Appendix (iv)) it is impossible to estimate its relative importance.
Further analyses were therefore carried out in respect of the most
strongly interrelated factors in order to establish the degree of unique
influence which each appears to exert.

Table 5.3 lists the factors which are interrelated at better than 0.4
as measured by Cramer's V statistic.[1] It must be noted that, although
these are the most strongly interrelated of the factors, they are not
necessarily the most influential.

---

[1] Cramer's V is a measure of interrelationship derived from the chi-
squared statistic. Its values range from 0 (no relationship) to 1 (perfect
relationship).

Table 5.3: Interrelationships between factors

Staff—pupil ratio with:	Cramer's V
School architecture: junior	0.51
Curriculum organization: junior	0.50
School architecture: infant	0.47
Curriculum organization: infant	0.47
School architecture with:	
Curriculum organization (junior)	0.49
Curriculum organization (infant)	0.44

For 'continuous' data, multiple regression techniques may be used to determine the uniqueness of the influence of related factors. Unfortunately, the use of these powerful statistical techniques with the dichotomous and categorical data typically yielded by questionnaires is inadmissible. Instead the data were submitted to repeated three-way contingency analyses.

This method operates by pairing the factors in different combinations, and for each pairing, examining the influence of one within each level of the other (i.e. with the other held constant) then vice versa. This was done with each of the 13 measures of school and classroom-based parental involvement included as Question 10e.

The results of this somewhat clumsy process are summarized as Table 23, Appendix (iv). A 'significance score' for each factor within each level of its 'partner', was calculated, representing its unique, or residual influence on aspects of Question 10e.

Table 5.4 presents the results of these analyses, in the style of an 'American' tennis tournament.

School architecture emerges as the strongest underlying influence amongst this group of interrelated factors. Very little of the variation apparently due to staff—pupil ratio remains statistically significant when the effects of architecture are first taken into account, whereas vice versa, the effect of architecture remains very substantial. Next in order of underlying influence is curriculum organization, the significant effects of which, though fewer than those due to architecture when paired with that factor, remain substantial in number. When paired with staff—pupil ratio, the effects of curriculum organization predominate in infant schools, but these factors are more or less equal in independent influence over parental involvement in junior schools.

Table 5.4: Underlying influence on parental involvement

	Contingency	'Score'	'Independent' Variable
Round 1	Staff–pupil ratio (infants) versus	1	School architecture (infants)
	School architecture (infants)	17	
	Staff–pupil ratio (junior) versus	2	School architecture (junior)
	School architecture (junior)	11	
	Curriculum organization (infants) versus	7	Curriculum organization (infants)
	Staff–pupil ratio (infants)	3	
	Curriculum organization (junior) versus	6	Staff–pupil ratio (junior)
	Staff–pupil ratio (junior)	7	Curriculum organization (junior)
Round 2	School architecture (infants) versus	13	School architecture (infants)
	Curriculum organization (infants)	8	
	School architecture (junior) versus	15	School architecture (junior)
	Curriculum organization (junior)	8	

Although these, and the group of three measures of social class discussed at the beginning of this chapter, show the strongest interrelationships amongst the various factors influencing parental involvement, the real extent of their relationships, each to the others, is modest, the strongest only reaching 0.51 (Cramer's V). Each therefore exerts a substantial measure of influence unique to itself. This is even more the case with the other factors, in respect of which the interrelationships are more tenuous. It is therefore legitimate to draw up a rank order of influence for these factors in terms of the number of types of school and classroom-based parental involvement which each significantly influences.

In terms of overall influence, the most important factors are parental occupation, school location and staff–pupil ratio (in junior school). The first two in importance are measures of the social class of the community served by a school. The expectation at the outset that the

Table 5.5: Rank order of influence on parental involvement

Factor	Number of types significantly influenced	
Parental occupation	10	
School location	7	*Strong*
Staff—pupil ratio (junior)	7	*influence*
School architecture (infants)	5	
Curriculum organization (infants)	5	
Staff—pupil ratio (infants)	5	
School size	5	
Head-teachers' incumbency	5	*Moderate*
Staff turnover	4	*influence*
School architecture (junior)	4	
Pupil turnover	4	
Free school meals	4	
Behaviour problems	3	
Curriculum organization (junior)	3	
Church connection	3	
Pupil's ethnic origin	2	*Weak*
Working mothers	1	*influence*

influence of parents' social class would predominate is thus borne out. Most of the other factors are moderately associated with parental involvement, confirming the opinions of those consulted early in the project. The two exceptions to this are (perhaps surprisingly) pupils' ethnic origins and working mothers.

Parental Involvement and LEA Policy

Many of the head-teachers consulted during the early stages of the project suggested that the prevailing policy of their local education authority had influenced them in determining the extent and variety of parental involvement in their own schools. In order to assess how far this is so for primary schools in general, a letter was sent to all LEAs, asking about their policies regarding parental involvement in their schools. The letter contained questions enquiring about guidelines given to head-teachers regarding relationships between school and parents, about LEA run schemes to promote closer relationships with parents, about courses for teachers and/or parents designed to increase mutual understanding and cooperation, and about school-based community schemes run by agencies other than the LEA. Replies to the letter were content analysed and a chart produced, detailing the extent and variety of policies adopted by the 70 per cent of LEAs who responded. The chart showed a wide variation in LEA practice, though there were no systematic differences between counties, metropolitan districts and London boroughs. For the purpose of comparison, 30 LEAs were selected from the chart, 15 with policies encouraging parental involvement (PI+) and 15 without such policies (PI−). Counties, metropolitan districts and London boroughs were all represented. Analysis reveals no significant relationship between LEA policy and the provision of after-school clubs or care facilities, the opening of facilities for use by the community, or the making of home visits by teaching staff or other agencies. LEA policy is significantly ($p = < 0.01$) related to levels of school-based parental involvement (Question 10e) for the infant and junior age-ranges but not for the nursery one. In both, levels of parental involvement are higher in PI+ schools.

Other measures of parental involvement to which LEA policy was found to be significantly related ($p = < 0.01$), included provision by the school of a room set aside for parents, publication of a school newsletter, election or co-option of parents on to the school's Board of Managers and the sending home of written reports concerning children's work and/or behaviour.

All but one of these measures are positively related to LEA policy encouraging parental involvement. The one exception concerns the inverse relationship between LEA policy promoting parental involvement and the sending by their schools of written reports to parents. One possible explanation of this unexpected result is that school reports are only sent, and only need to be sent, in schools where face to face contact between parents and teachers is minimal. In schools where parental involvement is actively encouraged by the local authority, reporting on children's progress might well take place more informally, by word of mouth, thus obviating the need for a formal, written report.

It is, of course, impossible to determine how far policies towards parental involvement adopted by individual LEAs are influenced by initiatives already taken to involve parents by their head-teachers. It may be speculated, however, that a higher level of parental involvement may be found among LEAs where these initiatives are actively fostered and encouraged to flourish, than among those where they are not.

Chapter 6

Case Studies: Schools and their Settings

The previous chapters have drawn upon a certain amount of the material from the case studies to illustrate the results of the national survey. The case study schools were introduced in brief on p. 28. This chapter is intended to serve two purposes; first to indicate more clearly the local features and environment of these schools and secondly to provide the background to the views of heads, teachers and parents which follow in Chapters 7 and 8.

The Nurseries: Riverside and Mill Street

Riverside nursery was situated in the middle of a small home counties market town in part of a converted private house. The play area also served as the staff car park and the main gates had to be kept locked as they opened on to a main road. The school, like many other nurseries, took children from a much wider catchment area than the town in which it was situated. Between 50 and 60 children attended daily; the children divided between the morning and afternoon sessions. Over 100 were on the waiting list. The children's backgrounds were extremely varied, ranging from the son of a wealthy stockbroker to the daughter of an unemployed labourer. This nursery, like many, had a fairly high proportion of children with problems, particularly speech or emotional difficulties.

The house itself was very old, and whilst the cloakrooms were on ground level the nursery itself was at the top of a flight of stairs. Water play took place in the kitchen, painting in an adjacent corridor and all other activities in one main first-floor room.

This obviously necessitated very careful organization and the staff rearranged the room frequently according to the needs of the children. Groups were regularly taken downstairs to play outside and frequent visits to places of interest in the locality were arranged. The head, a qualified teacher, worked closely with two nursery assistants, both NNEB trained, as well as with two NNEB students who each spent alternate weeks at the nursery.

There was a very wide range of activities available considering the limitations of the building and the head ensured that these were used to the full in her dealings with parents. She showed many dubious parents what play was, and explained what realistic expectations for a 3-year-old might be. She encouraged parents whose children had problems to discuss their progress almost daily and, if necessary, she maintained contact during school holidays.

Mill Street nursery was situated near the centre of a large Midlands industrial city. It was housed in a big redbrick building converted from an old secondary school, which it shared with a teachers' centre. The school was large compared with other nurseries visited by the team and comprised three generously proportioned interconnecting classrooms arranged in a straight line. They were nominally devoted one each to language, art and domestic work and in addition, leading off them at one end, the school had a utility room and a playroom equipped with large toys and a record-player. A spare room next door to the head's office was used as a parents' room. It had a table, chairs, equipment for making tea and coffee, and it served as a place for parents to meet, gossip and socialize.

The headmistress, Mrs Wilson, had had many years' teaching experience in a variety of settings. Her staff consisted of three nursery teachers and four NNEB trained nursery nurses who shared responsibility for the 70 full-time and 10 part-time children. Just under one-half of these children came from Asian or W. Indian backgrounds.

The nursery had a large catchment area embracing some of the most 'deprived' and decaying parts of the city. There was much multi-occupation, with few council houses. A transient population contributed to a high turnover in the school roll. There was no waiting list to enter the nursery, partly because not all the parents who were entitled to, made use of it. Consequently an effort was made to encourage local families to bring their young children to the nursery, amounting almost to 'touting' for business. As it was, in certain special cases, children were admitted from the age of 2 where it was felt that the home circumstances merited this, or when the school had been specially approached by the social worker dealing with the family concerned. Both head and staff realized the problems faced by the children in their charge and gave equal weight to the social and cognitive aspects of their education. As is the usual practice with nurseries, parents of new children were asked to introduce them to the nursery in easy stages over a period of at least three days, staying with them in the classroom until they seemed happy to be left on their own. An outline daily programme was pinned up on one of the classroom walls but this was used as a general guide only. Both children and parents were encouraged to call all staff by their Christian names, with the single exception of Mrs Wilson, the head. The staff found that first names were much more easily pronounced by children whose first language in many cases was not English, and that their use encouraged a warmer, more friendly relationship with parents.

Contact with parents was seen to be fundamental to their children's education. A home-liaison worker was attached to the school part-time, her wages being paid by the Cadbury Trust. Much of her time was taken up by liaison between parents and the local social service agencies and following up children who had for no apparent reason failed to turn up at the nursery for a week or so. Occasionally her job entailed such unusual activities as arranging bail for the father of one of the children. Relationships with parents were generally very good, with the head taking time and trouble to talk to them when they brought their children to the nursery in the morning, trying to persuade them of the important role they themselves played in their children's education.

As many of the parents were Asian and the mothers spoke very little English, a special class had been established for them meeting for two hours every Wednesday morning. Mrs Adams, the peripatetic teacher who taught the class, explained that there were 11 mothers registered, six of whom came regularly. They were generally willing to learn and were given homework, especially in the school holidays. One of the Asian parents, Mrs Singh, also acted as an assistant to the home liaison worker and interpreter for the other Asian parents. Many of them looked on her as a source of advice and counselling, in dealing both with the school and the social services. She also helped to run a weekly coffee morning to which people brought their problems, or came just for a gossip.

During the period of the case study there was another very interesting development in relationships between parents and the school. Every

Thursday morning a group of mothers gathered in the nursery play-room, while the children were variously occupied elsewhere, and began learning a variety of arts and crafts such as macramé, pottery, photography, etc., under the guidance of two or three workers from the local community arts centre. By the final visit this group had become firmly established and even those mothers who had been initially bullied into going by the head, seemed now to be really enjoying themselves. They were delighted to discover capabilities they had not realized they possessed and were proud of their new-found skills.

The Infant Schools: Blenheim and Elm Road

Blenheim Infants' School was situated in an urban area of Greater London. The three-storey, redbrick building housing the school was over 100 years old, had limited playground space and no grassed areas. It was surrounded by rows of small terraced houses most of which dated from the 1870s. The same building housed both infant and junior schools. The infant school occupied the ground floor and part of the first floor while the rest of the space, including the 'attic' rooms, was taken up by the junior school. Although the building was shared, the schools formed separate units, and the heads appeared to have different views on parent participation. The headmistress of Blenheim Infants, Mrs Thomas, was concerned to bring parents into the classrooms and school generally but this was not the attitude of the junior headmaster. The contrast between the schools was frequently commented on by parents in the sample who expressed anxieties over how their children would cope in the junior school and over the physical inaccessibility of the junior school's classrooms. The junior school had a large library on the shared first floor and Mrs Thomas had made several unsuccessful requests to the junior head for the use of a corner in this library.

The infant school's classrooms were of traditional layout, opening off the halls on the ground and first floors, and of generally depressing aspect, being short of storage space and in need of decoration, factors which could not be disguised by teachers' valiant attempts to brighten the walls with children's work. The hall on the infants' ground floor was fairly large but space was restricted due to the tables and chairs stored in it ready for lunchtimes when infant and junior children dined in relays.

There were approximately 190 children at Blenheim infants about 25 per cent of whom were of Asian, West Indian or mixed origin. There was a low staff–pupil ratio, there being a headmistress, seven full-time class teachers, a full-time 'floating teacher' and two half-time teachers who took remedial groups. There were also four 'ancilliaries' who worked in a rota helping class teachers either in the classrooms or in the staff room with routine jobs or educational acitivities under the teachers' guidance. The school was organized on traditional class-based lines with each teacher having her own children and room. The 'lower' infants (5- and 6-year-olds) shared six vertically grouped classes, while the 7-year-olds used the three 'top' classes on the first floor of the building.

The population served by the school was mainly skilled or semi-skilled working class, living in solidly-built terraced houses. The latter were all once privately rented but were now available for purchase on mortgages. The outer catchment boundary included some modern council maisonettes as well as large Victorian properties. The school was not designated as being in a social priority area but the head-mistress estimated that 25 per cent of her children had in-school behaviour problems due to their families' social and economic problems. Mrs Thomas and her staff had organized evening workshops for parents on reading and mathematics methods but the response from parents had been disappointing; so too, was the attendance of parents at open evenings. A few teachers had had some success in drawing mothers into the classroom for regular activities such as needlework but others had not, even though the majority appeared willing when interviewed. One mother, skilled in pottery, had come regularly to the school to take small groups and would then take the children's pots home for firing in a kiln which the school had helped to purchase. This mother intended to continue helping at Blenheim as soon as her new baby was old enough.

Teacher—parent contact of a casual nature at the beginning and end of the school day appeared easier and more frequent when the children were in the classrooms on the ground floor; parents were reluctant to go up the stairs to their child's class particularly, it seemed, because the first floor was shared with the junior school.

Elm Road Infant School was situated on the outskirts of a small town in the Home Counties. The school was housed in an old, redbrick building that had been recently extensively modernized. The original classrooms had been altered to form three distinct teaching areas, to each of which were assigned two teachers and a welfare helper (NNEB trained). There were nearly 150 children on the school roll, divided equally between the three areas on a partially vertically-grouped basis;

the 5- and 6-year-olds being taught together in Areas One and Two, and the 7-year-olds separately in Area Three.

The teachers in each area varied their approach between cooperative and team-teaching. Responsibility for the children was divided between them and each had a 'home-base', a small room at either end of the area where they took their class registers and dealt with dinner money. In addition to the three teaching areas there was also a large hall and a small library/resource room used for language and remedial work.

There was a nursery close to the school, housed in a large, modern building. It had 60 part-time and four full-time children, fed two other schools besides Elm Road, and was administered separately.

The catchment area of the school was largely working-class and seemed equally divided between council housing and inexpensive private houses. About one-third of the school's intake was from a community of non-English speaking Italians, who had come to the area to work at the numerous plant nurseries. They tended to speak Sicilian or Neapolitan dialects rather than formal Italian, creating enormous problems for the Educational Welfare Officer, Mrs Goldoni, who, though Italian herself, found that the only language in which she could communicate with them was English. Some of these parents were illiterate even in their own language, and few were taking the trouble to learn English properly. They were initially rather suspicious of the school, though Mrs Goldoni had done much to reassure them in the past year or so, In addition, the school had 14 'travelling' children on its roll. Their parents were all travelling show people who 'wintered' in the area from October to April each year. The difficulties raised by these part-time or non-English speaking children, coupled with the 30 per cent who come from one-parent families or broken homes had resulted in the school's catchment being classified as a Special Priority Area.

The school's main contact with parents came when they brought their children to school in the morning or collected them in the afternoon. Parents were encouraged to take an active part in the organization of school bazaars and fetes as well as helping to some extent in general classroom-based activities. The deputy-head, Mrs Croom, also ran a 'Ladies' Evening' for mothers once a week. Though it had began as a 'Slimmers Club' it had since diversified its activities and proved so popular that Mrs Croom had seen fit to introduce a second evening to cater for the increased demand. Both the headmistress, Mrs Crane, and her staff felt parental involvement to be important and regretted the number of parents who appeared to take no real interest in their children's education.

The First School: Brunel

Brunel first school, situated in a large town in the Home Counties, was built about 15 years ago to cater for children moving into a large council estate. Originally the school population changed almost daily as new families moved into the area. Many of the children were from various areas of London and had different backgrounds. The existing deputy-head remembered the period well and described many of the early problems associated with the upheaval of so many people.

These were not for the most part relevant now — except that it seemed possible that some of the social malaise of the estate could be traced back to these earlier days, when little help seemed to have been given to the uprooted communities. Certainly, the area had a bad reputation locally; vandalism was common, and many of the families on the estate needed and received considerable help and support from the Social Services Department. The school was recognized as being in a socially deprived area and had been allocated two extra teachers who both concentrated on remedial work.

The school buildings were generous in size, with both a large hall and dining room, kitchens being shared with the adjacent middle school. The children were grouped by age into six classes, which were housed in good-sized rooms situated off two L-shaped corridors. The reception class was quite separate, both from the middle age-range and the nursery children. The two classes catering for the children going on to the middle school the following year occupied adjacent rooms and the two teachers concerned worked closely together. The middle-age classes varied quite a lot according to the individual personalities of their form teachers. The head allowed each teacher to work as she felt best and this policy, in some cases, caused conflict between members of staff. The general pattern of working, however, was fairly formal, with reading, writing and number work being done in the mornings and other activities in the afternoons. A new, quite separate nursery class was opened a year ago.

This nursery merits special mention because it was from here that so much contact was made with new parents. It had only been operating for a year, but the teacher in charge of it, together with a home liaison officer (who worked in this school and its 'sister' school two miles away) had made considerable efforts to meet new pupils and their families at home. It was hoped that this would in time influence future relationships between parents and the school to the advantage of all concerned, especially the children from difficult or broken homes, and those living under conditions thought to be stressful in the high-rise flats.

The head thought that as many as 50 per cent of the children (roll 180–200) had quite severe problems of one sort or another, and reported that many children took sleeping tablets and tranquillisers. But, overall, the school seemed happy and despite these problems, had a positive attitude towards the all-round education of the children in its care. Social training was seen as very important, and went hand in hand with normal school subjects.

The Junior School: Barchester

Barchester Junior School was sited close to a 10- to 14-year-old private housing development on the outskirts of a large city in south-west England. Barchester Junior and the companion infant school next door were modern single-storey buildings with separate playground facilities and extensive green areas. The junior school was connected to the infant school by the shared kitchen facilities, but had a separate dining hall. Little contact between infant and junior school was observed during the study. Three years ago four additional rooms with cloakroom and corridor areas had been added to Barchester Junior. The school had 12 classrooms, a kiln room, a resources room, a small room used by the remedial teachers and 'reading-mothers' and a large entrance hall, in addition to the usual staff rooms and offices. The original square hall appeared fairly small but had a raised dais and was not used for dining except by the teachers. During lunch hour the floor-to-ceiling doors between the hall and dining room were folded back making a large area and enabling teachers to see and hear the children. The children had the use of a covered swimming pool built two years ago in the sports complex situated near the comprehensive school and community centre, a short walk away. The junior comprehensive school was one of four local schools which, with the community centre, were financing repayment for the pool.

The school had approximately 380 children aged 7–11 on roll, organized into four year groups. Each year had three form teachers in separate classrooms making 12 full-time teaching staff in addition to the head. A half-time 'floating' teacher supported the staff by concentrating on remedial work with small groups or individual children.

The children in each year were 'setted' for mathematics and English into three ability groups and during the morning the teachers remained in their classrooms while the children moved around to be with the teachers taking their sets. In general the largest groups appeared to be of the highest ability; as many as 40 in one high ability English set, while the children needing most help were in small sets, for example 17 in the first-year lower ability maths set. This system appeared to work smoothly though some teachers claimed that it was sometimes difficult to hear children read.

The catchment area for Barchester consisted of well laid out modern estates. There was a variety of housing available, ranging from terraced houses to semi-detached houses or chalet-style bungalows. Many of the parents had been born in the country, had moved to these estates as young families and had stayed on until the present time. The impression gained was of a friendly community where most people, mothers certainly, had established friendships with neighbours and were reluctant to move. At the time of the study the area had a low-level of unemployment with the majority of fathers in full-time, skilled or semi-skilled, non-professional work and many mothers working full- or part-time in local or city-centre shops and offices.

Mr Weston, the headmaster, had worked hard over the last few years to involve parents more fully in the school. The Barchester Association had been formed two years previously and its members helped organize acitivities such as school fairs, social gatherings and other events of a fund-raising nature. The association was so called in order to demonstrate that members of the community other than parents of children at the school were welcome. Parental involvement within the school was highly-organized; the 50 mothers who went in to hear children read 'each week were carefully selected, timetabled and supervized by the teaching staff. The reading standards at this school were very high, and both the staff and the parents themselves appreciated the efforts of the 'reading mothers'. Parents had helped decorate the entrance area and corridor. This included an unusual mural, having a painted backdrop combined with glazed and fired pottery, leaves and flowers, plants in tubs and display shelves for the children's own pottery. The school thus presented an extremely pleasant aspect on entry, which was enhanced by the open courtyard area, clearly seen through the windows, which housed the school's collection of small birds, fowl, and small animals such as rabbits and guinea pigs. Children helped the caretaker look after these during school hours.

The Primary Schools: Carford and Tyler

The case-study sample included four primary schools but only two, Carford and Tyler, are outlined here. The others St Hilda's and Spiritus Sanctus, were church schools. Both had nursery units and other close similarities in terms of the number of children and staff; a comparative profile of these schools is presented in Chapter 9.

Carford primary was situated in a small market town in south-west England. The school was housed in a large redbrick building that once served as the local secondary school which many of the present parents attended. It re-opened as a primary school two years ago, comprising three distinct units, junior, infants and nursery. Its roll was steadily increasing and was near the 500 mark during the study. The main building housed the infant and junior departments with one infant class taught in a terrapin hut in the playground. The rest of the school buildings were scattered over a wide area with the separate nursery unit a full five minutes' walk from the main school building. Next to the nursery was situated the dining hall together with another, separate hall used for gym and assembly.

The junior department was organized into four separate year-group units, each occupying two inter-connecting classroom areas. The two teachers in each unit 'cooperated' rather than 'team-taught' but the classroom-link areas were jointly used. The infant department consisted of five classroom areas linked by a central corridor in addition to one more orthodox box-shaped classroom, and a terrapin outside. Each classroom had an alcove containing a sink and other provisions for messy play.

The school was also equipped with two rooms used variously for remedial teaching and audio-visual work, the latter being a speciality of the deputy-head, Mr Baker. The playground also accommodated the local teachers' centre, and education library. The nursery was small and at times rather overcrowded; it had 33 children on roll, seven of whom attended part-time.

The school catchment consisted for the most part of three large council estates all recently built. Indeed the estates were still expanding, hence the increasing school roll and the projected reopening of one or two of the small schools in the town, closed when Carford opened. The estates occupied a distinct area of the town and formed a physically tight-knit community without, it seemed, any accompanying community spirit. They were bleak and poorly provided for, with few shops, and no pubs or any other 'public' facility, though they were at their furthest over a mile from the town centre. Many of the parents had been born in the town or the area round it. Unemployment was high and many of the mothers without pre-school children worked full- or part-time to supplement the family income.

Conscious of the problems which faced him, the head, Mr Allen, had decided to concentrate as much as possible on involving the school in the local community. Attempts to encourage community interest in the school had included the holding of the school's Autumn Fayre in the covered market in the town centre (raising over £400 in the process) and the inauguration of 'Friends of Carford School' which, it was hoped, would have a wider membership than the more usual Parent Teacher Association. The full-time teaching staff at the school numbered 20 including a remedial teacher, Mrs Vernon, and a compensatory teacher, Mrs Knowles, whose job description included home visits to both new and prospective parents and a reduced teaching commitment. Many of the pupils were considered to have social or emotional problems which explains the importance Mr Allen attached to the pastoral aspect of education.

Tyler Primary School was a combined junior, infant and nursery school under Mrs Parker, the headmistress, and was situated on the outskirts of an industrial city in the west Midlands. The original school building, now housing the infant class, was built in 1870; it had a large vaulted main room and two smaller rooms where group work could take place. In 1968 a purpose-built, open-plan junior school was added to the site, and in 1973 a separate nursery unit was built. In all there were two NNEB trained assistants in the nursery and two unqualified assistants attached to the primary school.

Tyler primary was a designated Social Priority School and part of the Community Education Project initiated by the local authority. A full-time preventive social work programme was based at the school, funded under the Urban Aid Programme. Resources were provided through the Community Education Project with the stipulation that these were to be used to provide a community service. Recently a cash grant had been given to decorate and furnish an upstairs room in the old infant building for parents to use as a meeting place; this room was very attractive with facilities for making tea or coffee and a large 'swop-shop' store cupboard where clean second-hand clothes were kept for exchange amongst the parents. Under the Urban Aid Programme Tyler Primary was allocated extra teaching staff and the help of a full-time social worker. The headmistress, home-liaison teacher and social worker made home visits as a matter of policy, Mrs Parker visiting the parents of children whose behaviour was causing concern. During the study, for example, two children persistently ran out of school during the day while two others were taken from school by plain-clothes policemen in order to have their photographs taken following a week-end spent in pilfering and damaging property.

The catchment area for Tyler Primary was narrowly confined, being dominated by blocks of low-rise council flats interspersed with terraced council houses. A quick walk through the estate built in 1958 substantiated its designation as deprived and gave credence to Mrs Parker's assertion that it was 'the most rapidly developing slum in Britain'. Many of the blocks of flats were half-empty with boarded-up doors and windows. The city housing authority had begun rehousing the tenants. Externally and internally the accommodation was in need of extensive repair and decoration; damp walls and ill-fitting doors were common. The outlook for people living here was depressing since the few grassed play areas were littered with rubbish, footpaths, covered walkways and staircases fouled by roaming dogs. The few shops serving the estate had shuttered windows. Sixty per cent of the children at Tyler Primary were from one-parent families; unemployment was high among the (largely unskilled) fathers still living with their families; and over three-quarters of the children at the school had free school meals. The catchment population was not stable; families frequently drifted into and out of the area. At present the number moving away was greater than that coming in so the school had a falling roll of about 300 during the study.

Chapter 7

Case Studies: The Teachers' Perspective

This and the following chapter are devoted to an exploration of the perspectives on parental involvement of head-teachers, class teachers and parents. Pooling of the information gathered from the eight case-study schools described in the previous chapter will, it is hoped, lead to a clearer expression of the similarities and differences within each group, and also highlight the extent to which each group's views converge or diverge.

The location, catchment, size and internal organization of these schools differed considerably (see the chart on p. 28). The survey had suggested that these factors have definite implications both for the extent, and the form of parental involvement.

1. The Head-teachers

Heads' own beliefs about the desirability of affecting closer links between home and school and giving greater opportunities to parents to express their opinions in school affairs are circum-scribed by what they see as strong misgivings on the part of teachers and perhaps over-zealousness on the part of parents. (Cohen, 1970.)

The head-teacher's position may often place him in the unenviable position of acting as representative, both of teachers to parents, and of parents to teachers. His personality and outlook may thus become crucial in deciding the nature and extent of relationships between the school and its parent body. The head of one of the schools where the questionnaire had been piloted was aware of the problem of teachers' and parents' mutual distrust and described the situation in her school thus:

> Many of our teachers are young and inexperienced, therefore self-conscious and reluctant to have parents in the classroom, though quite willing to have them help outside it. What the parents want and need is to be in the classroom, so the aims of the two are not truly reconciled, and it is difficult for parents to realize that patience is needed, that helping around the school might be a necessary stage for teachers before accepting them into the classroom. When staff changes take place the new teacher is faced with an established situation she does not really approve, and the parent may unwittingly make her feel 'the new girl'. Both parties are unable or unwilling to communicate their true feelings to each other or to the head teacher, so parents drift away, possibly feeling resentful and the exercise may prove to have done more harm than good.

In this, as in other situations, the efforts of the head in the interaction of seemingly opposing viewpoints may be critical to the success of the school's parent–teacher relationship.

1(i). The role of the parent

The head-teachers generally hoped that parents would support the school in what it was trying to achieve and make an effort to understand its aims and methods. The heads of Elm Road infants and Mill Street nursery both stressed the important role played by parents as the first teachers of their children. Mrs Crane of Elm Road explained:

> I think that parents don't realize that their children start learning from the moment of birth. These years are so important because they are the formative ones and children are with their parents for almost five years before they come into school. In that period they have to give their children secure, happy and stable backgrounds because this is when the foundations are laid.

If parents are seen in this light, then inviting them into school becomes merely an extension of their role as primary educators of their children.

The head of Barchester, Mr Weston, put it rather differently:

> The way I see it is that we have their children here and are obviously connected with parents in this way. If you ignore one

end of the relationship, i.e. the home, then you are a fool. Most
teachers who are also parents have felt dissatisfied and powerless
to do anything in their children's schools, often simply because
their support wasn't asked for.

Do parents, then, have a *right* to be involved in their children's
schools? The head of Carford primary appeared to believe so:

> Parents pay for education and very often they try to equate this
> with a business, talking about an end product and viability and
> all the rest of it, but at the same time I do believe that parents
> have a right to know what we're doing in school, why we're
> trying to do it, and I also think they have a right to come and
> help us if they are so minded.

1(ii). Parents and teachers

Notwithstanding their desire for parents to be involved in their
schools, heads were fully aware of the necessity of winning the support
of their staff for this although the manner in which they attempted to
gain this support varied from school to school. Mrs Crane claimed that
it was the teachers who invited the parents in to help, though with her
approval and encouragement. She felt that since it was they with
whom the parents would be working, it was only fair that her staff
should have the final say on who came in, what they did and for how
long. The head of Riverside agreed, underlining as well the need for
young teachers to be helped to deal with and achieve satisfactory
working relationships with parents:

> I personally feel that it is the head's job to give the necessary
> confidence to the young teachers under her. The only way to
> approach this I believe, is to show the teacher that you think
> very highly of them as a teacher in the first place. I feel their
> first year or two is not at all easy in any case, and parents can
> make this impossible without a lot of support and help. The
> young teachers I have seen with parents have had little idea of
> how to relate to them. They do not know how to use parents
> who do come into the nursery. Both parents and teachers are
> equally awkward and ill at ease. In a situation like this the head
> must intervene and put everyone at their ease.

However, not all the heads were as sympathetic. Mr Weston of
Barchester Junior had a much more pragmatic approach, explaining
that he did not want any staff in his school who did not want to be

involved with parents. In general, misgivings expressed by teachers in the case study schools were often dismissed by the heads or, occasionally, ignored. In any case it is true to say that they all believed that their staff, if not happy about having parents working in their classrooms, were at least prepared to tolerate them. The teacher–parent relationship will be discussed further in the second half of this chapter (pp. 97–109).

1(iii). Parents in the school

The reason why heads wanted to involve parents varied according to the location of the school.

Mr Weston, head of the school in the middle of a private housing estate, initially viewed parental involvement as a means of averting the serious effects of the cut-backs in educational expenditure of 1976:

> Over a year ago, in view of the economies, we sent a questionnaire to all parents, asking what (a) skills, (b) time they could offer the school. The response was so good that a member of staff has, as part of his work, to liaise with parents. He keeps detailed records of offers and within minutes can, for example, supply six mothers to make and serve coffee for a visiting Youth Orchestra.

However, although parents were first seen as a reserve to be tapped, other benefits arising from their involvement soon became apparent:

> The other point is that it fosters good relations between parents, staff and children. The committee of the Barchester Association[1] is drawn from a body of parents who represent other volunteer parents. It is quite tightly knit and promotes better parent–staff relationships and staff to parents relationships, also between child and parents because they understand each other's roles more clearly.

Mrs Crane of Elm Road Infants was also interested in parents for the help they could give, especially with such activities as sports days, harvest festivals, Christmas parties and fund raising, suggesting at the same time that the parents could gain much from this involvement.

However, it was not enough simply to send out invitations to parents to come into school to help; something had to be organized for them to do when they arrived. Faced with a totally new situation, and with only

[1] See Chapter 6, p. 84.

their own half-remembered experiences of school to fall back on, parents might well feel at a complete loss unless the class teacher could make clear exactly what was expected of them. Mrs Askew, head of Riverside nursery, repeated some advice she had given a young teacher friend:

> I was asked recently by a young teacher 'What on earth can I do with the parents? I have to have them in my classroom because the head says so, but I just don't know what to do with them'. I suggested to her that the first thing she did was to tell the parent to sit down so that he or she felt anchored and part of the classroom setting. Once they're sitting down children approach them naturally and the whole situation is immediately eased. I then feel it is important that the parent be asked to do something positive. Even if you don't need brushes washed or paper cut up, those first few moments in a classroom will determine whether or not that parent ever comes back. This is the crunch, because to feel needed is the most important thing a parent needs to feel in any school.

The head of Brunel first school also realized the importance of 'occupying' parents who had come in to help, even being reduced on occasions to asking parents to water the plants distributed at various points around the school.

The importance of providing suitable employment for those parents who volunteered to help in school was put in a wider context by Mrs Donna Johnston, the Training Advisory Officer of the Volunteer Centre, Berkhamstead. She told a conference on the Recruitment, Training and Support of Volunteers:

> The plea that we need volunteers is going to sound awfully hollow if they turn up and there is no work for them. I remember when the media — on its own, with no consultation with us — announced during a flu epidemic that hospitals needed volunteers. Floods of volunteers turned up when the professionals were barely able to cope as it was.

She went on to explain how futile volunteering must have seemed to these people when they realized that no-one had enough time even to tell them what they could do to help and there was, finally, nothing they could contribute. This vital point will be dealt with at greater length in Chapter 8.

1(iv). Parents' problems

The role of 'parent counsellor' adopted, at least in part by large numbers of head teachers has already been referred to in Chapter 3. The heads of the case study schools were also aware that many problems could be solved or avoided by sparing time for a chat with parents. The questionnaire data revealed a significant relationship between social class of catchment area (as measured by parents' housing and occupation) and the likelihood of heads adopting a counselling role, with heads increasingly likely to be called on in this respect in areas of poorer housing and by parents in unskilled occupations. However, even in the mainly middle-class area of Barchester Junior, Mr Weston found that many parents turned to him for advice:

> They mention personal problems if these are linked with the child, such as a death in the family or the problem of a father drinking. The stability of school life can act as a good buffer for the child when home life is difficult.

He had misgivings, however, about spending too much time in counselling parents, wondering about problems that could arise if there was an amateur 'Citizens Advice Bureau' set up in the school.

In contrast, the head of Tyler Primary, Mrs Parker, worked in a catchment area consisting of a socially derpived council estate. Her reasons for involving parents in the life of the school were couched more in terms of what the school could do for the parents than what parents could do for the school. As part of a wide ranging community development scheme run by the local education authority, Mrs Parker entered whole-heartedly into an open-school policy. Parents were welcome at all times in the school to sit with their own children or work with groups of children. Mrs Parker was always willing to talk to parents who came to the school to discuss their personal problems as well as the educational problems of their children. Mothers could be seen pushing prams through the classrooms and generally about the school during the day. Mrs Parker aimed at establishing informal contacts with parents in the hope that this would break down their fear or dislike of schools, nurtured in their own school days, and encourage their confidence in helping with their children's education. She saw this as having educational and social importance as much for the parent as for the child. She explained:

> There has been up to the present time very little of giving on the

part of parents. Most of them come in because in some way they need help. Training in self-help is a long process and we believe ourselves to be in the midst of it. Perhaps if we were asked for our basic aim, it might be to make some small break in the cycle of deprivation.

Apart from the parents' room which had been set up in the old part of the school Mrs Parker also hoped to set up a clinic at the school at which the nurse could advise parents about seeking further medical advice for their children, as very few took them to the one located some distance away.

The head of Mill Street nursery, Mrs Wilson, considered that the school had an important part to play in helping the parents as well as the children:

> I definitely feel that I take on the whole family. First of all the parents are allowed free access to the school at any time they want and if the children either aren't very successful or have difficulties then we discuss this with the parents too. We see how we can best help both the child and the parent, trying to reinforce the parents' own self-confidence or give them confidence in the first place, reassuring the parents that they can handle the child and all they have to do is to use their common sense.

She saw her role as head of an inner-city nursery as being much wider than just that of an ordinary class teacher.

> I believe if you can see education as more than just what takes place in the classroom, and if you've done your years in teaching, then in fact you are ready to see it in a different form. By educating parents, in fact, I am educating the whole school. I feel very strongly, and the inspectors feel this too, that the head teacher's job is much wider now than it used to be, not limited to organizing and leading the teaching in the classroom.

Although Riverside Nursery was set in a prosperous Home Counties town, a high proportion of children on its roll had problems or emotional difficulties. The headmistress, Mrs Askew, felt she had an obligation to help parents with problems, her approach to parental involvement being very similar to that of Mrs Wilson:

> I have always believed that the child cannot be looked after on his own. He's part of a family unit, and if there are difficulties and problems he must be looked at as a member of a family not just as an isolated individual.

> Because I see the mother and child as a unit, I believe it is very important that the mother be brought into the nursery whenever she wants to be there along with her child. If a mother has a problem with a relationship between herself and her child I do believe it's my job to help her with it. If the mother has a problem it will inevitably affect the child. It is therefore also our responsibility to help that mother with any problems she may have, if we are able to do so. It may be that she feels inadequate, or insecure, it may be she has a bad self-image. I feel that the nursery setting, because of its special family environment, is ideally suited to helping her resolve any difficulty she may have.

Mrs Askew was committed to the view that school and parents should work together as closely as possible for the good of the children. She used the nursery environment in a therapeutic way and undertook on several occasions to act as counsellor to parents with problems, accepting them daily into the nursery for this purpose, one case lasting over 14 months.

Heads have to bear in mind the needs and responsibilities to both parents and teachers in any attempt to bring the two together. However, it is the head-teacher who more than any other single person, acts as the lynch pin of parent—school contact and it must therefore seem strange that so few local education authorities provide any form of training for their prospective or newly-appointed heads in management or human relations. Only three heads were encountered who had been given any training at all, even short in-service courses, the prevailing opinion being that heads would have acquired the requisite skills 'on the way up'. Their increasingly important role as parental advisers and counsellors underlines this deficiency, with a number complaining that the advice they can give is limited by their lack of expertise and information. The school's increasing importance as a source of advice and help for parents with problems will be considered both in the following section and in Chapter 8.

2. The Class Teachers

During the Autumn Term of 1977 and the Spring Term of 1978, interviews were conducted with 70 teachers and five nursery assistants in the eight schools considered here. The interviews were semi-structured and took an average of 30 minutes. A minority of interviews were recorded in longhand when the use of a taperecorder was prevented by adverse conditions, such as background noise and frequent interruptions when interviewing was carried out in the class-room or outside the open classroom door. In some cases, where it would have been possible to use tape-recorders some teachers refused, saying that they did not want a 'permanent' record made.

The class teacher is the person who has actually to put into practice in the classroom all her own or her head-teacher's theories about parental involvement. Teachers thus have to find a satisfactory resolution of interests encompassing these theories as well as their own interests as educators, the parents' concern for their children and the demands of classroom life and curriculum organization. Teachers have to come to terms with any disparities and find practical solutions.

2(i). The role of the parent

Teachers distinguished between the role of parents in the home and their role *vis-à-vis* the school. Most made the point that parents should try to provide a stable home environment for their children, to give them a 'good' upbringing and to care for them. A Barchester teacher summed up:

> Parents are the main influence on their child. They inform and discipline their children. They should provide a secure home background.

A teacher at Mill Street agreed:

> Well, parents are probably the most important people in their children's lives. I think it is their responsibility to bring them up socially aware and to give them a good start in life, to teach them as much as they can and generally see if they can bring them up to interact with other people successfully, peers and adults.

However, many teachers also acknowledged the gap between their ideal of responsible parenthood and the reality they were faced with from day to day. They complained that children were sent to school still unable to use a knife and fork, to go to the lavatory unaided and, in exceptional cases, even to walk or talk properly. The apparent assumption on the part of parents that the school would accept responsibility for their children's social as well as cognitive education, was seen by some teachers as an abrogation of the parents' own responsibilities in this area. A teacher at Carford complained:

> I feel that infants still need a mother figure and that infant schools are taking on more and more of the responsibility for children once exercised by their parents. They ask me to teach their children table manners and the more I do as a teacher the more I am expected to do. One parent told me today that her daughter had hurt her ankle yesterday evening and asked if I could put a plaster on for her.

Views on the parents' role in their children's education varied according to the age range of the children concerned. At nursery and infant schools, teachers frequently stressed the important part parents can play in the pre-school and early school years in the child's development of language and social skills:

> Parents should try to supplement the work we do at school by talking to their children about what they've done here and just taking an interest, because a lot of children who come in don't seem to have had anyone to talk to them very much. A lot of the children have a very poor vocabulary for their age and children whose parents do talk to them and do discuss things with them stand out. A lot of parents seem to miss opportunities to talk to the children and help them develop in that way. (Teacher at Elm Road infants.)

Teachers of nursery and infant children emphasized the help parents could give to their children's total social and intellectual development. This emphasis declined as the children progressed through the junior school. Fewer teachers of junior school children spoke of the value of parents reading or talking to their children, but referred rather to the value of parents showing a general interest in everything they did in school and coming to school, when necessary to sort out any worries their child might have. The elaboration of the curriculum as children grew older thus influenced the contribution to education which teachers thought parents should make.

2(ii). Parents in the school

Nearly all teachers interviewed stated that they liked to see parents in the school building. However, this general view was coloured by qualifying statements relating to the time that parents appeared and their purposes in coming. At nursery and infant level teachers often saw parents when they brought their children to school or when they collected them in the afternoon. A reception class teacher at Carford explained:

> I certainly like to see them first thing in the morning, I like to hear anything they've got to say about the children. I like to see them again in the afternoon so I can tell them anything that's happened to the child during the day.

Teachers also felt it was a good thing that parents should come into school to discuss particular problems:

> Generally I like to feel that parents are free to come in about problems with their child, that there is no barrier between teacher and parent, that they don't feel they only need to come in to complain but that they can come in just to have a chat. You gain parents' confidence slowly. It's a three-way system here and I think the parents should see the head first and not just wander around the school aimlessly.

Barchester Junior was unusual in that it organized Dads Army evenings whereby fathers met with staff members at the school for one evening every fortnight to do repairs or help make equipment required by staff. This was seen as very useful for social reasons as well as the material benefit coming to the school. A teacher explained:

> To my mind the 'Dads Army' evenings encourage closer contact with parents in after-school hours. I have found that they are very dependable people and it is valuable to get to know parents from a social point of view.

Although teachers generally wanted parents to come into school they felt there should always be a clearly defined reason, or purpose, for doing so. This attitude possibly stemmed from a desire to retain a measure of control over the activity of non-professionals. At Tyler primary some teachers explicitly stated that a completely 'open' school was not to their liking and the reasons given sometimes pointed to the disruption which parents caused while teachers were trying to teach and fears that parents would sometimes be in a position to abuse confidences:

> There should be firm guidelines laid down, then parents would know where they are and so would the teachers. Parents shouldn't be using the staffroom unless invited in by a teacher, but now they're in there on their own. They can see confidential

information on the board, I don't think this is right. The fact that parents can come into the staffroom is resented by other staff or at least by quite a few of them. There also seems to be a constant stream of parents coming through the (teaching) areas with pushchairs and interrupting the lesson. Parents have been known to walk through the room swearing at each other as they go. This is very difficult when you are trying to read a story, for example, to the children.

This point of view certainly highlights the conflict of interests which can arise when a head has a long-term view and pursues an 'open-school' policy without the complete confidence or understanding of all the staff members. Those in agreement with the teacher quoted above felt themselves to be in an invidious position. They were not 'against' parental involvement but disagreed with the way it was being initiated and implemented by the head:

I don't really want parents in my classroom because I don't like the basis on which they bring them in, in this school. To my mind parents should be brought in for specific reasons and aims. Now they seem to be in for non-specific reasons; often all day they are sitting around. (Previous speaker.)

The situation developing at this EPA community school was giving rise to uncertainty among the teachers as to what exactly the aims were as regards parents. They expressed concern for the parents' position:

There are dangers if the parents don't know what they are in school for and it can be just a waste of time. I like to have parents in for specific purposes. Parents can't be much help or gain much by taking a passive role. They have to be really involved. Very often they are seen wandering around here and don't seem to be doing anything. (Teacher, Tyler Primary.)

And for their own position, even when committed to the value of involving parents:

I am very much in favour of parents in schools. Having them in school generally and being able to invite them into the staffroom at break is something I like. Not many come in but certainly some do. This can give rise to concern... I don't mind them coming in but there are times when you want to go into the staff-room and blow your top...if a kid has driven you to despair... or, it could be that you are having problems with a member of

staff and want to tell another member of staff about it. I feel
then, that with parents or outsiders in there, one can't do that
and it can be frustrating. I don't know how you get over this
problem. (Teacher, Tyler Primary.)

The problems which can arise due to conflicting interests and
expectations were at their clearest in this open-plan, community
school. The head had taken the long-term view with regard to parental
involvement. Through her commitment to an open-door policy she
hoped that the barriers between parents and school would be broken
down and that once parents became familiar with the school and
staff they would begin to take a more active helping role. Many of
the teachers were primarily concerned with the day-to-day business of
running their shared areas and although the majority were in favour of
involving parents, they were not in agreement over the steps taken to
achieve this. The majority wanted structured parental involvement and
felt that this would relieve their own uncertainty as well as that of the
parents. This school was exceptional in that at least two parents
regularly went into the staffroom without specific invitations and
teachers were often unsure as to why they were present.

The desire of the Tyler staff for a structured involvement of parents
was echoed by teachers in other schools, though not as explicitly
perhaps, because few others were facing a similar situation. In fact
an interesting contrast may be made between the views of teachers
at Tyler Primary and those at Barchester Junior. This school had a
highly organized formal involvement of parents during the school day.
Most of this involvement took place outside the classrooms in the
entrance hall or small reading room where mothers heard children read.
Parents were canvassed for their support at the beginning of each school
year and one teacher was responsible for compiling a list of volunteers
on whom teachers could call. Fifty parents each week came to hear
children read and because of the number involved, they were timetabled so that each teacher knew where and when parents were attending. All teacher appreciated the help given by parents and favoured this
clear structure for involvement. However, a number pointed to certain
difficulties which could arise when the involvement of parents was
highly structured from a central base rather than determined by the
individual teacher and parent. The more experienced teachers often
said that, while the volunteer lists and parent timetabling might be useful for those new to the school or to inexperienced teachers, the system

wasted valuable weeks at the beginning of each school year while the arrangements were being made. Furthermore the times at which parents were scheduled to come to the school were not always convenient for the teacher concerned. One teacher summed up the difficulties:

> This is the only school I have been in where parents are involved in a full-scale organized way. At my previous schools mums would come in if you, as a teacher, particularly asked them to do so. To be honest I would prefer to do it myself at this school. It is four or five weeks into the term before mums come in to hear readers. I don't think this is the organizer's fault but merely the fact that it is so formalized. There are also the problems of trying to fit mothers in with the classes that teachers have planned. When I first had a 'reading mum' it was not at a convenient time. I rearranged my timetable to try and accommodate the mother but after a time I could see it was just not going to work. I then rang the mother and asked if she could come at a different time. (Teacher, Barchester Junior.)

The teachers recognized that with so many parents coming into the school during the week, they could not all be involving their particular parents at the same time. Only the most experienced and confident of teachers would risk suggesting alteration to the carefully organized presented timetable.

Thus, notwithstanding the good intentions of both Mrs Parker at Tyler and Mr Weston at Barchester, the relationship between teachers and parents was not always an easy one. It must be made clear, however, that the organization of parental help at Barchester generally appeared to work well and indeed many teachers admitted that they relied on parental support for such educational activities as school trips, craft work, and general help and supervision while they worked with small groups.

The difficulties encountered at Tyler were perhaps all the more regrettable as the socially deprived nature of its catchment area might suggest that it was precisely here that good parent—teacher relations were most needed. The support offered to parents by the head must surely have been undermined by the difficulty her staff had in backing her up, leaving the parents more than a little unsure of the kind of welcome they might expect if they took up Mrs Parker's rather vague invitation 'to come in and help'. This problem will be discussed further in the next chapter (see p. 125).

2(iii). Parents in the classroom

Many views were expressed by teachers regarding the involvement of parents in classroom-based activities. Views on a suitable classroom role for parents varied according to the age of the children taught. At nursery level, for instance, their help and cooperation was highly valued:

> Parents can be a tremendous help, especially if you are short staffed. I could do with them in today; they can help with extra special things. For example, today we are having a birthday party for one of the children. They can help children change and dress. An extra pair of hands is always useful.

The nursery staff recognized the close relationship between mother and child and were willing to utilize this to help the child settle or, alternatively, help the mother over the separation by providing company at the nursery. Also the range of social and intellectual skills which make up the nursery curriculum is highly similar to those operating in a good home.

At infant level, particularly at the lowest age, views were similar. For those children who had not attended nursery or playgroup, entry to infant school is the first transition for mother and child. Thus many infant teachers were happy to see parents bringing their child into class in the mornings and to accept or ask for parents' help:

> I have a parent coming in regularly on Tuesday afternoon. I give her a group of three to five children. They do needlework as this needs special attention. I give her these small intimate groups and this is good also for children with language problems, so that they can just talk, especially if they are withdrawn or shy. A one-to-one situation helps.

Infant teachers frequently mentioned 'individual attention' as one advantage of having parents in the classroom, working with children. They varied, however, in their views of activities for which it was possible to recruit parental help and were generallly divided on the question of using parents to hear children read. Many did not want them to hear readers, particularly if they were poor readers. Reading was clearly a major educational matter in respect of which the teachers were concerned to exercise their expertise. These teachers were more guarded in their approach to having parents working in their rooms:

> It depends on the parent. An obviously sensible, intelligent mum can sit and hear reasonably fluent readers. I wouldn't give any parent anything which involved teaching a new idea. They come to *help* and the children see them differently, they see them as a mum. They could do reading or number games but not a brand new topic such as introducing a sound in a teaching situation.

Another infant teacher wondered what her qualification was worth if she allowed untrained parents to do her job. She added:

> I feel that language and story are very important with infants. The teacher must, as part of her skills training, know what is an appropriate achievement for each child. To do this you need continuous contact over time and a parent or helper does not have this; they cannot see the pattern the teacher has developed.

This speaker wished to safeguard her area of professional expertise, believing this to be in her own and her children's best interests. Such a view was echoed by many infant and junior teachers. Among the latter, however, reading was less of an issue. It was, in fact, one activity in which parents were thought to be capable of contributing a great deal. At Barchester, teachers were unanimous in praise of the mothers coming in to hear the children (these mothers sat outside the classroom and teachers sent the children out to them). They were, however, consistent in their views that parents should not be allowed to hear children with reading difficulties and that careful supervision was required at all times:

> Remedial readers stay with their teacher or the remedial teacher. Careful checks are made on each child who goes to a parent for reading.

The older the child the more teachers appeared to take the view that parents should not be allowed to teach basic skills in school. They stressed instead the benefits of parents helping with craftwork, needlework, pottery, junk modelling, or maintenance tasks, clearing up, cutting up paper or covering books, and hearing fluent readers. The main justification for not enlisting parents' help in the basic learning processes seemed to be that parents were not trained for the job and could cause confusion:

> I would rather they come in and just talked to the children than try to do teaching. If they're going to attempt any of the definite

technique side, then I think they need help, because you can confuse children so easily. Even two teachers in a team situation can do things differently and the kids have different ways of learning and that's enough without other people coming in on top.

This is a major problem mentioned by many teachers with regard to parental involvement. It is the problem of knowing where to draw the line between 'teaching' and 'non-teaching'. An associated difficulty was discovering what parents were capable of. At some schools the teachers were willing to enlist parents' help but at a loss as to know what they could do if the parent was illiterate, innumerate and also unable to offer much practical help to children. At schools in 'deprived' or difficult areas where teachers wanted to establish better relations with parents and foster mutual cooperation, there was the immediate problem of enticing parents into the school and the delicate matter of finding what they were capable of doing if they did come in. Teachers felt that they did not always have the time to train parents even for simple tasks and, where they had taken time to encourage and welcome a parent, they often felt let down when the parents did not come back, or came so irregularly that it was difficult to organize things for them to do.

However, in a number of cases attempts had been made to find suitable activities for even apparently the most inept parent. Thus in one school that did not have an afternoon break, each teacher in the mid-afternoon received a cup of tea from a mother who was very happy to be able to help in this way. At another school a semi-literate mother revealed an ability to make very attractive models out of ordinary clothes-pegs. Teachers at both these schools were convinced that the efforts made to involve these parents in the life of the school were fully justified.

Another area of concern for many teachers was the effect of a mother on her child when she helped in the same class. Sometimes the child would behave in such a way (often badly) as to gain attention; at other times, mothers were over-anxious and at one infant school a teacher became worried because a mother persistently checked and corrected her own child. Many teachers (nursery teachers were the exception) were wary of allowing a child to be with his own mother until they had acquainted themselves with both parents and child. At a school where parents helped children with reading, cookery, music, art, needlework, and, more generally, by supervising children undressing and dressing for swimming, a teacher said:

> There are always problems but I think the main one I've come across is the over-anxiety of parents working in an area near their child. It made the child rather tense as he could never get away from mum or dad as one of them seemed to be in the school with him a lot of the time. It depends on the parent, though. With our 'cooking-parent', we've had her daughter last year and her son this year and you wouldn't know they were connected.

This concern was raised by many of the teachers interviewed. Some said that under no circumstances would they have a mother helping them if her own child was in the class; others were willing to experiment, to see how parent and child would react and ask the parent to help in another class if difficulties arose.

However, not all those parents who might have liked to help, were able to, either because they worked during the day or because they still had a pre-school child to care for at home. This occasionally resulted in another problem, expressed by one junior teacher, thus:

> We've got one or two mums who have actually felt left out. They feel that if they came in and gave more time to helping in the school it would benefit their child, but it doesn't really work that way. They feel that they have to go out to work and they can't come in to school, yet if they don't come to school, then in some way their child misses out. I don't know whether it's an attitude that stems from mum herself, or whether it stems from the child who sees someone else's mum come in to help and wonders why his mum doesn't come in. I feel sorry for them.

Interviews with parents did in fact bear out this teacher's concern. Those unable, or not wishing to go in to school frequently expressed mixed feelings on the subject of parental involvement. This will be dealt with more fully in Chapter 8 (p. 118), since it is perhaps illustrative of the parents' focus of interest on their own children, an interest which is parallel but not coincidental to that of the teachers.

In spite of all the problems encountered in asking parents to come into the classroom to help, the vast majority of teachers interviewed stressed that the benefits deriving from parental help far outweighed the difficulties experienced. After they had accustomed themselves to working with another adult in the room (by no means an easy thing for those used to working in a 'closed-box' classroom with the door kept firmly shut) they often came to rely on parents' help, whether this was hearing children read, or merely helping them dress following a PE lesson.

The question of the physical presence of other adults in the classroom was clearly one with which teachers have difficulty in coming to terms. No teacher expressed a wish for parents to be in the classroom all day and every day. One teacher, committed to involving parents for their own sake as well as for that of their children in a severely deprived area, said:

> There are times when you want to be on your own with your class. This helps to build up a learning situation where the children respond to you and you to them. This is more difficult if parents are present.

So, even if some parental involvement in the classroom was seen as beneficial, more involvement was not always seen as better. Teachers need to build up relationships between themselves and their classes and, while a certain amount of parental help might facilitate this, too much might well impede it.

2(iv). Parents' problems

The questionnaire data indicate that 80 per cent of head-teachers spend time in counselling parents on social, domestic or marital issues. The heads of Tyler Primary, Mill Street and Riverside Nurseries saw their role as being directly concerned with such parent counselling as a necessary part of the education of their children. This prompted an interest in whether a counselling role was also being adopted by teachers. Teacher reaction to our questions regarding giving advice to parents varied according to the age and/or experience of the individual teacher and the kind of catchment area in which their schools were situated, since this determined to a certain extent the number of parents requiring help.

Generally the older the teachers were, the more prepared they were to give advice to parents on matters not directly related to the education of their pupils. It seemed that the older, married, woman teacher was approached more frequently by parents having difficulties at home, whether economic or domestic. Some teachers saw their response to parents simply as a natural consequence of their own humanity and not a response that was necessarily connected with their role as teachers:

> Yes it is part of my job to advise and counsel parents especially on educational matters, but on domestic difficulties too. You

can't isolate the child from its family and as a person, you should never close the door to another person's problems.

Such teachers clearly saw the child as a product of his environment who could not be dealt with in isolation. Disturbances at home were seen as directly affecting the behaviour of children at school.

It is part of my job to advise parents who come for help if it is something relating to the child's behaviour in the classroom. But so many of these things are connected closely with home and you've got to be so careful that you're not seen to be meddling in their home affairs. With the best will in the world you've got to be terribly careful round here, especially where you've got so many broken homes and so many problem families.

Teachers at schools in poor areas were frequently approached by parents for help and tended to be aware of the economic and social deprivation of the children in their classes. Having faced these situations they had experience which was obviously lacking among teachers who had remained in schools in wealthier areas with a minimum of social or economic problems. The teachers in deprived areas were clearly re-thinking the nature of their involvement in education:

If you had asked me that some years ago the answer would have been 'No'. But now, in this school, I do feel it is part of my job to advise and help parents. We sometimes involve parents more for their own sake but ultimately we feel that if we can help them we can help their children. I think that the parent can sometimes build up a relationship with the child at school and it is this which is frequently missing in the home. (Teacher at Tyler.)

The younger teachers at such schools were also responding to parents' needs, but their attitude was somewhat ambivalent as to whether this was a proper activity for them as teachers. They often remarked that they lacked experience and were not trained to counsel parents:

At parents evenings, obviously, parents sometimes come in and say, 'so and so is really worried about school. What can I do to help?' You talk about it then. I think if it's to do with the child, and if it affects the child's happiness, then it will affect the child's performance in school. But if you're talking about advising mum whether she should go off and leave dad, I'm not trained for that sort of thing; I'm not a social worker.

This caution on the part of teachers concerning a counselling role also manifested itself in the one case-study school located in a notionally middle-class area (Barchester Junior):

> In a personal situation, I can only advise on my own experience and only play a sympathetic role. Really, I can't give guidance. My chief concern under those circumstances is the child.

Few of the teachers we interviewed thought that training was vital in dealing with parents. It was thought to be more a matter of common sense, of having a 'sympathetic ear', or of having experience of life:

> I don't think you can train a teacher how to talk to parents; I think he's got to know what it's like to work side by side with people, all sorts of people, not just his own type. I don't think it's a thing that can be taught at all; you have to learn it by jumping in at the deep end. You have to learn how to get on with people and surely this is what we're trying to teach the kids all the time.

While this was a common view with regard to initial training, some teachers felt that in-service training courses might be beneficial; they would gain far more from such courses once they had had the experience of learning at first hand about the problems faced by parents and the exact type of help they needed. Others said they would need information on the appropriate agencies with whom parents could, or should, be put into contact if they were going to advise them properly:

> I think it might be beneficial to have some knowledge of social services, to have some answers that you could give to parents, because when they come in they either want a sounding board where all you've got to do is listen, or they want information which we haven't got. We need to be able to contact someone when the parent comes in, to be able to hand them on to some-one else, because ultimately we are an education system and our greatest disservice to the children is if we forget this and let them go by the board, trying to solve the social problems.

A teacher at one of the case study schools had definite misgivings about the role of counsellor he had been forced to adopt by the many parents who approached him for advice:

I feel that this shouldn't be part of the job, but it definitely is, here. I get parents coming to me asking if I'll have a word with their child because they are rude at home or they get into trouble. Basically, I try to avoid making myself available for this kind of work; after all, we have got a social worker here who is more suitable and trained for it. Certainly, it is part of our job to advise parents on educational matters. We have 'open nights' and discussions and they are always asked if they want to see how we operate in a classroom. They can help their children, then, at home.

Certainly, many case study teachers were worried that the demands made on their time by parents impinged unjustifiably on the education of their children. Such comments as, 'The children must always come first', and 'I was trained as a teacher, not as a social worker', expressed the ambivalence shown by many teachers to their responsibilities to parents as well as to children.

It would appear, then, that these teachers, while recognizing all the benefits accruing from the involvement of parents in their children's education, had certain misgivings, first about the integrity of their professional status and secondly about the expansion of their role to include parental counselling. Recent talk of cutbacks in school staff as a consequence of falling rolls and economic stringency have made teacher unions all the more vigilant to safeguard employment opportunities for their members. The use of parents to perform duties that might be better carried out by unemployed teachers may well lead to bad feeling; in fact the project team came across one school in which parental involvement had ceased following a union directive. Thus teachers may occasionally find themselves in the invidious situation of wanting to involve parents in the life of the school on one hand, while on the other doing their utmost to protect the professionalism of their educational role. The expansion of this role to include parental counselling and advice has also provided many teachers with cause for concern. While feeling out of common humanity that they cannot ignore parents' pleas for help, many teachers may still find it difficult to judge how much time should be spent in advising parents, time which might be put to better use in educating their children. The resolution of these potential conflicts must surely be a matter of concern for educational decision-makers at all levels.

Chapter 8

Case Studies: The Parents' Perspective

In the previous chapter parents and parental involvement in primary schools were viewed from the teachers' perspectives. That of the parents is now considered.

Interviews with 140 parents (a 10 per cent sample) took place during the Spring term of 1978. Those interviewed were randomly chosen from each school register. This ensured that they were a representative cross-section of the population which each school served, including both those who were already in some measure involved in the life of the school and those whose contact was negligible, even non-existent. Parents were initially contacted by letter and the interviews were subsequently conducted in their homes.

It had been intended at the outset of the case studies that where possible both parents would be interviewed together. However, this proved impossible in many cases as the only time both parents *were* at home together was during the evening. Though many evening interviews were conducted, pressure of time necessitated that the majority were carried out during the day, when usually the mother alone was present. It is felt that this is no way invalidates the results of the investigations as even when it was possible to interview both parents, it was most often the mother who appeared the better informed about the school and the child's experience of it.

When asked if they were willing to take part in the study, parents were generally welcoming and quite happy to talk. It did not prove possible to contact all the parents in the sample even after calling on them on three or four separate occasions, but the 140 interviewed still represented over 90 per cent of the original sample. There were only two outright refusals, both from parents of travelling children at Elm Road Infants whose general distrust of authority clearly extended to educational researchers.

Interviews were conducted along similar lines in all cases, based loosely around a semi-structured schedule. The questions were deliberately left open-ended, providing a focus for discussion about parents' views and feelings rather than a fact-finding enquiry. The intention was to seek information concerning parents' knowledge of how their child spent his or her day at school, as well as about their own relationship with the school and its staff. The questions were evolved following consultation with teachers at the case study schools and pilot interviews with a number of parents. They are reproduced here as headings under which views expressed by parents are loosely organized.

On the whole parents said they were happy with their children's schools and satisfied with the education they received. On those occasions when hostility or dissatisfaction was expressed, complaints concerned antipathy to individual teachers just as often as to teaching methods or curriculum organization.

Q. (i) What does your child say, if anything, about what he/she does at school? What do you think he/she does all day?

Parents generally learnt little from their children about the school's educational activities. Children it seems, told them about unusual or exciting things that had happened during the day, e.g. moving on to a new reading book, starting a new project, but very little concerning the general everyday life of the classroom. This lack of information did not appear to worry parents, however. A parent from Blenheim Infants said:

> They are very vague really. It hasn't worried me; the eldest was the same and now she brings work home from the juniors. The youngest brings home paintings and we collect boxes for their projects. I find out what they are doing when I go to see the teacher.

Another agreed:

> You can go on parents' nights ... The teacher takes the time to talk to you. I think I know enough.

In fact, parents appeared to know little of what their children did at school, the curriculum and the teaching methods in use. Even the

better-informed of those interviewed confessed to difficulties in understanding the 'modern' teaching approaches adopted by their children's
schools:

> I don't really understand; it is entirely different now, especially
> the arithmetic.

As a rule parents from more middle-class areas seemed better
informed than those from working-class areas, particularly the socially
deprived. Parents of nursery children also tended to know more about
their children's day than did parents of older children. In spite of the
attempts at parent education made by such schools as Tyler and
Carford Primaries, few had any real idea of how their child's day was
organized or what actual work they did. A number of parents at Tyler
admitted to being confused:

> I always thought that children sat down, read and wrote at
> school, but now I'm not so sure as they come home and say they
> have had a film show.

None of the parents at Carford attributed any value to infant play
and one or two sharply criticized the amount of time infant children
spent playing. In addition, comments from a number of parents concerning the adverse effects of Carford's open-plan design on their
children's ability to concentrate seemed to be founded more on an
intuitive distrust of modern teaching methods generally than on any
real evidence as to how their children's work was actually being
impeded.

Understandably, parents who had been into their children's school
to help seemed to have a clearer idea of what their child did and of the
organization of the classroom. A mother from Blenheim Infants
explained that when she had first gone in to help, it seemed a 'very
disorganised routine' but after a while she could see 'that there was
quite a structure there'. The children sat in groups, she said, and were
required to do three pieces of work: reading, writing and number,
after which they could choose what else they wanted to do. This parent
pointed out that the 'choosing' was between educationally planned
activities, e.g. Lego, clay, but this provided 'a sugar lump' (her words)
for those who were slow to complete their work.

Another mother, whose child attended Mill Street Nursery and who
was herself a trained infant teacher, agreed:

I think, seeing what was going on in the nursery and the way the teachers dealt with the children, I was amazed to see how much the teachers could get out of them. I am really thinking of art work because there is a product at the end of it; the children's art work has been fantastic and seeing the different things that they've been doing, it's opened my eyes. I used to think of painting, model making with junk material, clay and perhaps a bit of pasting and sticking; I thought that was it. But here they use a lot of materials and the children have really improved.

Q. (ii) Who do you think is responsible for your children's moral upbringing?

Answers to this question generally concerned the teaching of manners and morals, which was the responsibility of the home, and the setting of standards of discipline, which was the joint responsibility of the home and the school. Nearly every parent felt that discipline was the school's responsibility inside school time and were concerned that children would be allowed to do things at school that they were not allowed to do at home. A few parents at Carford thought that school discipline could be improved by the use of corporal punishment while others confessed ruefully that their children took more notice of their teachers than of them.

Certain parents thought that once the child was at school the responsibility for up-bringing (in all ways) should be shared by parent and school; they felt a joint effort was needed to maintain good behaviour and that parents should keep teachers informed of any problems and vice versa, so that both could take appropriate action.

One parent at Blenheim Infants mentioned her responsibilities regarding her children's education:

Parents' main responsibility is to encourage the child as much as they can at school . . . I impress upon mine that the harder they work now, the better they will do; then they won't get dead-end jobs when they leave.

Similar views were expressed by other parents interviewed.

Q. (iii) How do you think school and parents can best cooperate to help the child?

The majority of parents were in favour of increased home–school cooperation for the sake of the child. However, views varied as to how best this increased cooperation might be accomplished.

The parents at Blenheim were grateful for the chance of seeing teachers when they collected their children from school in the afternoon, particularly when they had something they wanted to discuss. Reasons given by Blenheim parents for 'getting together' with teachers varied:

> Parents should go in, otherwise they don't know what the children are learning.

> The better you know the teacher, the easier it is for that teacher to say frankly that a child is a beast in class and for you to work (together) to help get over it.

The PTA also provoked mixed reactions, with some feeling that the committee attracted 'the wrong person'; for example, 'those who want to be on *any* committee'. Parents who were, or had been involved with the PTA commented that it was useful for discussion on how to help the children but meetings were infrequent and poorly attended. Other parents felt that they could help at home by talking and listening to their children, though they were occasionally afraid that they did it 'differently to the school'.

Certain parents appeared a little more diffident about approaching the school. Unexpectedly, this was as true of the middle-class parents of Barchester, as of the socially deprived of Tyler. Many of the former felt that open-evenings and attendance at school functions would ensure increased home—school liaison while others wanted closer involvement. Their concern was expressed in comments such as:

> We don't get a lot of information on what they teach... We had trouble understanding the maths methods.

> I don't feel you can go down (to the school) just to put your point of view. You can't make an appointment to do this... it doesn't seem a proper reason for going.

These parents were reluctant to appear at the school in order to ask for information on specific teaching methods in case they were thought to be criticizing the teachers. They believed, in common with many parents from other sample schools, that 'causing trouble' or 'interfering' would 'be taken out on', or otherwise adversely affect their child.

Parents at Tyler Primary were as anxious as those at Barchester to promote good home—school relations. As one mother put it:

> In my day we were just left at the gate; a child takes more pride in what he is doing if a parent takes an interest as well.

Mothers of children in the nursery at Tyler said that the toddlers' group held one afternoon in the week was a good way of getting to know teachers, other parents and their children. They felt reassured seeing their own child among others of the same age since they could see how they compared in terms of behaviour.

Most of these parents mentioned open evenings as a useful way of discussing their children's work in private but, although they claimed to be able to visit the school for open evenings, or at any time during the day, it was clear that few did so. Many parents excused themselves on the grounds of having a job or young children still at home, but others told of the difficulties they experienced in discussing their children's progress with their teachers:

> I don't know what to say to teachers or I forgot what I wanted to ask. It's in your mind but it's different when you try to say it.

Certain parents clearly felt that teaching was best left to teachers, a feeling possibly arising from their inability to recognize the influence they themselves might have on their child's learning:

> Personally I think that if they can't be taught at school they can't be taught at home ... they do their work totally different to the way in which I was taught and I couldn't show them in the same way as their teachers.

Q. (iv) What do you want the school to do for your child?

Parents generally wanted their children to receive 'a good education'. Though opinions varied as to the form 'a good education' might take, it usually included a thorough grounding in reading, language and number; except, that is, for parents of nursery children. Parents at Carford, Brunel and Elm Road Schools hoped their children would be given a good education to help them 'get on in life'. One or two also hoped they would be given a better education than they themselves had received. Parents also wanted the school to prepare children adequately for the next stage of their education, whether it was junior or secondary school. One unusually articulate mother from Tyler Primary felt strongly about this:

> The school should prepare them for the secondary changeover. The one fault I can find with Tyler is that they don't seem to do this very well...Jane found it hard to adapt from the teacher—pupil relationship at Tyler, where it was personal and friendly, to the relationship at Woodway where there were different teachers for different subjects and a far more formal day. My point is really that the methods of teaching are so different at the two schools that the children become confused when they go up.

Parents from Barchester hoped that, in addition to providing a basic formal education, the school would help build up their children's social competence, their personality and generally prepare them for their future life:

> They should try to help them express themselves properly; if the teacher takes time now it will help later on.

> As long as he proves himself to be well-behaved and respectful and able to cope with current affairs and his future life, I'll be happy.

> A comprehensive all-round education, varied not specialised; something to inspire them for the future.

> To spark off their imagination so that they will follow it up. That's when parents can come in and back up teacher's efforts.

Parents of nursery children saw nursery experience as providing companionship for their children, broadening their experience, and preparing them for infant ('proper') school. Parents from Mill Street Nursery said they had sent their children there initially so that they would have somewhere to play and children of their own age to play with. The children, they said, had acquired a wide range of social and cognitive skills, varying from learning to use a knife and fork, to being able to write their names. One mother claimed that bringing her child to the nursery was 'the best day's work I ever did'.

Q. (v) Would you like to know more about school activities? How would you like to find out?

The majority of parents interviewed felt reasonably well-informed about school activities, often as a result of the frequent newsletters sent out. Parents also said that if they had anything in particular they wanted to know, they could always 'go and ask the teacher'. Of those who wanted to know more about school activities, many said that education had changed completely since they were at school and they found great difficulty in understanding modern teaching methods. If they could in some way find out more, especially about the English and maths schemes, they would be better equipped to help their children at home. Many of these parents suggested that one means by which this could be accomplished would be by inviting them into the classroom to watch the teacher and children at work:

> They could invite parents in once a week so that you could be there while they're actually teaching, showing them the mathematical system — binary is it? — this foxes me!

At least half the parents at Barchester said they would like a written report to show them how their children were progressing. Parents were only allowed a brief meeting with their child's teacher at open evenings (some parents were clearly afraid of over-staying their welcome on these evenings and did not like to stay past their allotted five minutes); a written report would prepare them for the meeting and they would have more idea of what questions to ask regarding their child's progress. One mother, regretting the passing of the 'old fashioned itemised reports', said:

> Now I have to ask exactly how the children have done for everything and I feel sometimes that you could be left with the wrong impression about your child.

Q. (vi) Are you nervous about going into school?

Any nervousness experienced by parents when first visiting the school seemed to have been partly related to their own fears about meeting a new set of people, and partly to an anxiety as to how their own child would cope with the school, the teachers and the other children. Most said that whether or not they had been nervous to begin with, they were perfectly at ease now and found the teachers approachable and easy to talk to.

However, at Barchester a number of parents were still apprehensive when visiting the school for open evenings 'About what they might be going to say about my child'.

> If I have to meet the teacher I'm always afraid he will say Mary is the opposite to what I think she is. I know how hard she tries at

> home and how she feels, so if I go expecting the teacher to say
> she doesn't try at school, I feel nervous... There's a barrier
> between teachers and the parent really. They don't see your child
> as you do.

> I find it awkward to mix, expecially at schools. I'm a bit nervous
> of the teachers, they seem to be in a class of their own.

> I think the worst and am worried before I get there.

Q. (vii) If invited would you like to help in school in any way?

Well over half the parents interviewed said that it would be impossible for them to help in school time because they either had young
children at home to look after, or a job. Many of these, however, did
help with bazaars, summer fetes, etc., either by helping to organize or
run them or by making things that could be sold. One or two parents
from Blenheim Infants said they would like to help in the classroom but
would not push themselves forward; 'I wouldn't want it to look as if I
was interfering.'

At Carford Primary there were mixed feelings about parents' help
being recruited for the classroom. It was felt by some that the school
could use parents' help in the classroom to spread the teacher's load
and ensure, for instance, that each child was allowed to read to an adult
at least once a day. Others were totally against the use of parents in this
way, claiming that they weren't trained to do the teacher's job. One
mother whose son was a 'slow reader' complained that he had not been
allowed to bring his reading book home whereas other mothers were
allowed to hear him read at school; this, she thought, was most definitely unsatisfactory. Parents who did help in the classroom were also
criticized for gossiping about other people's children.

Many of the Tyler Primary mothers did not go out to work and said
they would like to help in school. Most, however, added that they
would like to be *invited* to help.

> Yes I could help if I was asked. I could do cookery and I could go
> regularly; I'm here all the time.

> I don't feel I could just go into the class to see them working.
> I would want to be invited in for a specific reason, so that I
> wouldn't feel I was interfering.

Some parents appeared to need a direct and personal invitation to go
in to help:

> She never *says* you can go into the class.

> They never seem to want help, they've never asked me anyway. I would have helped if they had. I would willingly give a few hours a week to do cookery or needlework and help them make things.

Parents at Barchester were also aggrieved at not being asked to help, claiming they had offered their services by filling in a form but had not been called on. 'You are lucky, I suppose, if your name is picked out', one mother said.

On the whole, it was thought that it would help children if they saw parents around the school; it showed the children that they were interested. Of the few Barchester parents who helped in the school, only one felt it was very formal.

> I just go in, hear readers and come out. I don't see anyone much or get to know the teachers any better by going in.

Others felt they were very welcome in the school, that they got to know the teachers and that they, and the children, enjoyed having them there.

Q. (viii) Would you like the head or your child's teacher to visit you at home?

The large majority of the parents of children in the case study schools with the exception of Tyler Primary, saw no point in a home visit, saying that they could always visit the school if they had something to discuss, and that things related to school were better discussed there than at home. A minority of parents both at Mill Street Nursery and at Brunel first thought it might be a good idea for teachers to see how their children were at home and to gain an understanding of their relationship with their parents outside the classroom.

At Tyler the majority of parents were in favour of home visits, especially if there were problems with the child at school. They felt it would enhance teacher–parent relationships, and enable teachers to see those parents who could not visit the school. A few, however, thought that teachers already had enough to do and that visits to parents would be 'an awful strain for them'.

Q. (ix) Would you like the school to offer facilities for meeting other parents?

At two of the case study schools a specially designated 'Parents' Room' was provided, though attitudes towards its use varied. At Tyler Primary a few said they had not known there was a parents' room. After discussion it seemed that they thought the room was only for mothers with children in the reception class and since the combined keep-fit/coffee morning had ended they had not been back to the school. Other parents did not think that young children could go up to the room so they were unable to go themselves. All parents believed that the room was good idea, even if they themselves did not use it, since it provided a chance to escape from their home routine, meet other people and plan activities to raise funds or make things for the children.

At Mill Street Nursery, on the other hand, the 'Parents' Room' was in almost constant use, and parents welcomed the chance it gave them to meet other mothers. Many had found their attendance at the Thursday morning mothers' group a great help, both in getting them out of the house and in introducing them to new interests as well as to people with whom they could share them. One Asian mother said that before she had started coming on Thursday mornings she had been 'sick and tired of being at home on my own all the time'.

Many of those at the other six schools said that they knew other parents as neighbours and had also met them while taking their children to school or collecting them in the afternoon. One or two mothers from Carford suggested the school should hold a coffee morning or afternoon for mothers and toddlers. There were a great many lonely young mothers living on the estate, they explained.

Parents from Blenheim Infants would have welcomed a 'Parents' Room'. One mother explained:

> We usually stand around outside the school in little groups or on our own. Often on our own. We only seem to get together for functions, so it might be nice to have a room where we could go inside and sit.

Q. (x) Do you think the school could or should provide help for parents with problems?

Apart from those parents at Tyler Primary and Mill Street and Riverside Nurseries, it was generally thought that school could provide help for parents if their problems concerned their children but not where they were related to their own domestic circumstances. A few thought that teachers already had enough to do without being asked to cope with parents' difficulties and, in any case, they were not trained for this work and might do more harm that good. One mother from Blenheim Infants suggested that a social worker ought to be attached to the school, or shared between three or four schools in the neighbourhood. Teachers could then put parents with difficulties in touch with this person.

In contrast, parents at both Tyler and Mill Street valued the advice and help they received from the school very highly. One mother at Tyler commented:

> The school is, for a lot of people, the only place they go to other than the shops.

Parents at Tyler felt it much easier to approach the school if they were in difficulties, than a strange place they did not know. Sometimes all they needed was someone to take the time to listen. 'A friendly ear helps', as one mother put it. The help provided by the social worker attached to this school was praised by those families who had contact with him.

Parents at Mill Street Nursery also welcomed the help they had received from Mrs Williams, the head, and from the social worker attached to the school. One mother, the wife of the local vicar, explained how the school could, and did help:

> In this area a lot of parents have real problems; they are mostly single parent families and they know that this is a place they can come to if they want to talk their problem over, either with the headmistress or with the advice worker. The people in this area have to have somewhere that is handy — I mean, a young mother with young children can't just get on a bus and get into town, but they *can* come down the road here — I think it means a lot. From the point of view of the church, we like to think that people will come to us if they've got problems, but a lot of people in this area are working class and have a mental block about the church, especially the Church of England; they think it's posh, it's only for the posh people and this is the way they feel. The immigrants wouldn't come because we're Christians and they are not. So this place acts as a centre where they can come; they've got a contact through their children, anyway, and, because there is a friendly atmosphere, I think they do feel that they can come with their problems.

Two other contemporary studies (Tizard, n.d. and Grant, n.d.) have reported parental views of schools similar to those quoted. A study by Wilson and Herbert (1978) of 56 large, deprived families living in the inner city also supports the conclusion that parents, especially working-class parents, are ill-informed about their children's education:

> The majority had no views on the objectives of education; they were largely accepting, though not necessarily supporting, the educational system. Teachers were seen by many as authority figures whom they are prepared to back up in conflict situations. The majority of parents felt welcome when they visited school on parents' day. But at the same time less than one-third were satisfied with their somewhat tenuous relationships, and many commented on the absence of real dialogue; 'I haven't been as often as I'd like — anyway, you only see their work.' 'Teachers haven't the time'. 'They ask you not to go inside the gates, they might send for you if they are really worried.' 'When I went up I was wandering about like a fool, I didn't know where Wayne's work was.' 'I don't think they want much to do with the parents, I don't think they bother very much.' 'If father is out of work they make you feel low.' A small number of mothers had no contact with school: 'I never see them, I don't particularly want to'.

Wilson and Herbert's quotes from parents' interviews sound strangely familiar! It was found that though a few of those parents who actually became involved in classroom activities seemed to have a reasonably good grasp of the methods by which their children were taught, there was little evidence that parents in general understood the school's teaching approach, or felt they needed to. In fact few of the teachers in the eight sample schools saw parental involvement as necessitating parental education except in the widest sense of enlisting their support for the aims of the school, educational and social.

Wilson and Herbert concluded that increased parental involvement did not necessarily result in harmonious relations with school staff or improved functioning of children and in many respects the team find themselves forced to agree. In spite of the attempts made by all the sample schools to contact, involve, and generally build up good relationships with parents, they seemed to have had but little success in making them feel part of the educational process. The large majority of parents appeared to be far more concerned about whether their children were happy in school, whether they ate their school dinners, whether they 'fitted in' with their classmates; there was little time left for worrying about the methods by which they were taught, methods that are so different now to when they themselves were at school.

Parents often felt at a loss when faced with these methods, especially at Parents' Evening when they felt the need to ask 'intelligent' questions about their children's work. When interviewed, they consistently claimed that if there was anything they wanted to know, anything they were unsure about, they could always visit the school and discuss it with the head or class teacher. It was clear, however, that relatively few took advantage of this facility. In the course of the interviews three main reasons for this reserve became apparent. First, certain parents felt that their queries did not come into 'proper' areas of concern; that they were not 'legitimate' questions which they could expect teachers to answer, rather inarticulate feelings of unease and bafflement. Nor was this feeling limited to parents from working-class areas; thus the comment from a parent in middle-class Barchester:

> I don't feel you can go down (to the school) just to put your point of view . . . it doesn't seem a 'proper' reason for going.

Secondly, parents were often perplexed as to which questions to ask when they were unsure what they were asking *about*. Questions about Fletcher books bothered one mother interviewed; she was concerned not with their efficacy as a form of instruction in mathematics, but whether her daughter used them for reading, number or artwork! Thirdly, and related, was the inadequacy many parents may feel when faced with a situation in which they themselves experienced failure. One mother claimed a real interest in her son's progress at school, but confessed her own illiteracy made her feel completely inadequate to enquire about her son's reading and writing at parents' evenings. Though she felt she was in some way letting him down by not attending at the school's parents' evenings, she could not face the humiliation of confessing her disability to her son's teacher:

> They make you feel low if you can't get on with reading and writing.

Notwithstanding the sympathetic approach of the teacher concerned to other parents with this difficulty, this mother's view of school as a hard and unfeeling institution persisted and it was this which determined her reactions to it. Once attitudes become entrenched in this way, they tend to persist irrespective of whether or not they are based on a misunderstanding. One particular instance of this, encountered in the course of the case studies, concerned a petition sent to a head-master by a dozen or so parents complaining about the quality of the school dinners, a matter not strictly under his control. The reply, inviting the parents concerned to visit the school and sample the dinners for themselves served only to annoy them still further as, they pointed out, the letter had also asked for due notice of their intention to take up the invitation thus enabling the school 'to make a special effort when they know we're coming', as one parent put it.

Always in the background was parents' anxiety about 'interfering' or 'causing a nuisance' and the fear of the repercussions this might bring down upon their child. Even supposing this fear to be ungrounded, it still indicated the mistrust and incipient hostility of many parents towards both school as an institution and the teachers within it.

This mistrust may be linked to the differing perceptions of the child held by teacher and parent. This could constitute the crux of the problem. Many teachers said that they would be unwilling to have a parent help in their classroom if that parent's child was in their class. As one teacher put it:

> I think a parent would be too involved with the well-being of her own child in that class, unlike a teacher who takes care to en-compass all of them.

In other words the 'interested' attitude of the parent would be bound to conflict with the 'disinterested' attitude of the teacher. However, in spite of this conflict of views, it was the use of parents to help in school-based activities that appeared to be the most productive area of home—school cooperation. At the time of the project's inception, schools throughout the country were suffering from the effects of the Government's economic cut-backs which had severely affected many LEAs. Coupled with the reductions of school rolls due to a falling birth-rate, this had led to a cut-back in staffing and had prompted many head-teachers to look round for other resources they could tap. Mr Weston of Barchester Juniors had invited parents in to the school to fill this gap:

> Over a year ago, in view of the economies, we sent a question-naire to all parents, asking what (a) skills and (b) time they could offer the school.

They found that parents were often glad to help and had unsus-pected skills that could be utilized to enrich their children's education.

Thus parents not only helped to dress children after PE or swimming, sewed costumes for the Christmas play and helped clear up the classroom they could also teach the skills of pottery or needlework to children, give talks about their jobs, professions or any interests they had, to the whole class, and help with football and netball both in and out of school hours. Despite the many misgivings voiced by some of the teachers in the case study schools, most seemed pleasantly surprised at how well it seemed to be working. As the survey showed, a large number of heads (52 per cent) wished to expand this involvement, both in terms of increasing the number of parents involved and of diversifying the activities with which they helped. However, even the most enthusiastic head-teacher would find it difficult to involve more than 20 per cent of his parents in school-based activities without swamping the school with adults, so for the specific purpose of promoting home—school contact this tactic must necessarily remain of limited value. Another problem raised both by the Tyler Primary parents and the head of Riverside Nursery, concerned the need for specific and personal invitations for parents to come into school and help. The comment of a Tyler mother:

> I would want to be invited in for a specific reason, so that I wouldn't feel I was interfering.

would have been easily understood by Riverside's head:

> Even if you don't need brushes washed or paper cut up, those first few moments in the classroom will determine whether or not that parent ever comes back. This is the crunch, because to feel needed is the most important thing a parent needs to feel in any school.

However, parents may be involved as much for their own benefit as for that of the school. This leads on to the final area of home—school relations considered here; the role of the teacher as counsellor and adviser to parents in difficulties. The head teachers of three of the case study schools, Tyler Primary and the two nurseries, reported that a significant amount of their time was taken up in helping parents with problems not necessarily related to their children's education. The survey showed just how widespread this activity was: 80 per cent of heads reported spending time advising parents on social or domestic issues. To a lesser extent this was also true for the class teachers in the

case study schools and their responses to the demands made on them
in this way are discussed in Chapter 7. A measure of the success experienced by the heads of these three schools is revealed by the fact
that the majority of parents interviewed in each case claimed that if
they had problems they could not deal with themselves or if they
needed advice, they would turn to the school in the first instance.

As one of the conclusions to their study of disadvantaged children,
Wilson and Herbert (1978) look to the nursery to provide positive
discrimination to offset effects of social deprivation.

> Although there is no magic in the early years of development . . .
> nevertheless specific skills and behaviour can be helped in the pre-
> school in such a way as to prepare for initial coping with school.

They continue:

> Benefits to mothers as well as children may be a major aspect.
> Also the nursery can act as a social centre and a source of parental
> education.

In fact analysis of the questionnaire results revealed that a much
higher proportion of nursery head-teachers (94 per cent) spend time
advising parents on domestic issues, than head-teachers in other types
of primary schools. The growing importance of this aspect of the
teacher's work calls into question the precise nature of his or her part
in the educational process. It has been suggested that it could be
defined more appropriately as that of an 'educational social worker',
especially in areas where social and economic deprivation leads parents
to look to their children's school for more than mere teaching. The
extent to which teachers are willing to reconsider their roles in this
manner, and the extent to which LEAs are willing to encourage, or even
condone, are both matters for conjecture. What can be said is that in
some areas at least, advice on how to cope with marital breakdown,
even if it only consists of the addresses of the local Samaritans or
Marriage Guidance Councillors, may do far more to improve home—
school relations than any attempt to explain the advantages of the use
of phonics or ITA for the teaching of reading.

Chapter 9

Two Schools Contrasted

St Hilda's and Spiritus Sanctus Primary Schools were located within a mile of each other on the outskirts of a large industrial city in north-west England. They were both linked to Roman Catholic parishes and their wider than usual catchment areas overlapped at one point, both schools having children on their roll from the opposite side of the main road separating their two parishes. In many respects the two schools were remarkably similar. Both were housed in medium-sized, closed-plan buildings, each equipped with an integral nursery unit. The children, roughly 200 in each school, were divided between six horizontally grouped classes and the nursery. A falling roll had reduced their teaching staff and as a result each school now had one 'transition' class for top infants and bottom juniors. The hall, centrally located in each school, separated the box-like classrooms into infant and junior departments.

Apart from the fact that both heads had chosen class-teaching as the method of organization, the general approach to the curriculum in the two schools differed significantly. While Spiritus Sanctus had adopted the teacher-centred style more usually associated with its traditional architecture, St Hilda's, under the enthusiastic guidance of its headmaster, had steadily developed a more 'progressive' teaching approach culminating in the introduction of the integrated day. Notwithstanding this difference in approach, the academic standards in each school appeared remarkably similar, though it must be stated that this view is entirely subjective.

The two council estates from which most of the children were drawn were the outcome of slum clearance in the centre of the city. Though building was still going on, some of the houses dated from the early 1950s and most of the parents had been living in the area for five years or more. Many of the fathers were employed in semi-skilled or unskilled occupations either locally or in the city centre, though among those parents interviewed were also found a policeman and a data control analyst. There seemed to be little sense of collective identity and few parents knew many of their neighbours. This lack of community spirit might well have been due to their 'transplanting' from the tightly-knit communities in the city-centre slums. It certainly appeared to have affected their church-going habits as only half claimed to attend regularly, a situation of which the head-teachers of both schools were well aware. In fact, though both heads took seriously the role of their schools in instructing their pupils in the Catholic faith, religion was kept in fairly low profile, comprising morning assembly and a prayer at lunchtime and at the end of the afternoon, in addition to one or two lessons each week devoted to religious instruction.

Due to the location of the schools at some distance from the churches to which they were attached, there was little connection with the life of the parish, except on such occasions as pupils' First Communion or Confirmation. The head of St Hilda's regretted that the parish priest did not go more out of his way to contact parents and talk to them in their homes.

In spite of the many similarities between the two schools, the attitude of their head-teachers to the involvement of parents differed significantly.

The head-teacher of Spiritus Sanctus, Mr Ryan, was suspicious of any attempt to woo parents into the classroom, feeling that teaching in whatever form could only be undertaken by those properly trained to do it. His staff shared his opinions and some difficulty was experienced in winning their confidence and persuading them to be associated with this project. In all but one case at this school, teacher interviews were conducted without the aid of a tape-recorder. At St Hilda's, on the other hand, the head-teacher, Mr Riley, saw the involvement and education of parents as fundamental to the education of their children. He felt that teachers should 'come down off their pedestals' and treat parents with 'the respect they deserve'.

A sound basis thus exists to make a 'fair' comparison between these two schools of the contrasting relationship each had with its parents. Since the schools were similar in regard to location, architecture and size, it was thought that it would be their approach to the involvement of parents which would differentiate them in parents' eyes.

St Hilda's Primary

One of the most marked features of St Hilda's Primary was the atmosphere of the school. Staff and children appeared to relate to each other easily and on a friendly basis and this was especially true of Mr Riley, the head. Teaching styles varied with the age of the children but generally a rather structured form of integrated day seemed to be practised in the juniors and with rather less structure in the infants. Class teaching was apparent throughout, with classroom doors generally being kept firmly closed and no attempt being made at cooperative teaching. The friendly atmosphere of the school was, however, reinforced by the 'family dining' system at lunchtime.[1]

Mr Riley, the headmaster, was in his early forties and married with two children of his own. He began his teaching career in a Home Office Approved School in the Gorbals in Glasgow and had transferred to primary school teaching about seven years previously. At the time the project team first visited the school he had been headmaster there for three years. He was anxious to involve parents in the school as much as possible, seeing this as part and parcel of their children's education. He thought that parents were generally interested in their children's progress through school and above all in whether they were happy there:

> I would say that their youngster is their most valuable possession and I find this increasingly so from talking to parents; they are very emotional about their children. They are highly sensitive about how happy a child should be and they want to be seen to be friends with the teachers and the school generally. They want their child to see that mum can talk to you and talk to the teachers and be friendly and happy.

As long as the school was doing a reasonable job in educating their children, he thought parents wouldn't be concerned with the form the education took:

> No parent wants to tell a teacher how to teach; they don't give a damn what you do, that's not their concern. They want this

---

[1] There were two sittings for lunch and the children sat in groups of seven or eight at tables in the hall. An older child at each table was selected as 'table leader' and it was his responsibility to collect the food from the serving hatch and distribute it to the others. Roughly half the staff, including the head, ate with the children, and there was always great competition among them to have a teacher sit at their table.

happiness to exist for their child, and 'Can my child read well?'
is a secondary issue.

Mr Riley saw the mounting of fund-raising activities as the principal
method by which parents could become involved with the school:

> I looked at the parents in this school and asked myself, 'What
> can they do? How can we relate to them?' and our best way of
> relating is by running functions. Some functions we run, we don't
> need to make a profit; for instance we don't make a profit on the
> dance we run. It's a social function, purely for teachers to come,
> or managers to come and whoever they want to bring, and the
> parents and everybody, and we have a damn good time.

As far as parents helping in the classroom was concerned, Mr Riley
was of the opinion that this should only happen if the teachers involved
were agreeable.

> I won't impose any parents on any teacher, though I will encour-
> age it.

In fact parents helped in such classroom-based activities as hearing
children read, setting up tape-recorders for SRA language work, cutting
up paper, mounting children's work, etc. There were, however, certain
activities in which he felt it would be inappropriate for parents to be
involved.

> They must always remember that they are helping the teacher.
> I meet them and say, 'The teacher will usually advise you what
> to do.' I leave it to the teacher to say how far they can go.
> I wouldn't have them teaching phonics, for example, that's a very
> expert thing, I wouldn't have them teaching a whole class some-
> thing about number because this is a progressive thing and parents
> bursting in on it and confusing the youngsters would add more
> complications to our lives.

He felt that, though teaching the children remained his priority, the
school should be a caring community, with time made available for
parents and their problems. He was adamant that the efforts made by
him and his staff to involve parents were amply justified by the benefits
sustained:

> Yes, I think it's a tremendous advantage. In 1974, the year I
> arrived here, we had a reading test which is done in all schools in

the authority. The score for this school was 7.2, a bit low. At that time parents stood outside the school gates, they dared not come in. They never communicated with the school, they had to make an appointment to see the teacher, they never came to a social, there was nothing for parents. When it was open evening all the teachers met in the hall at a desk and all the parents went round in a ring and spoke to each teacher like at a cattle market. At the time of the '7.2 rating' the school was very formal and they were reading all day. Teachers will tell you that they did reading groups all day; finish one reading group, then start the next. In 1977,[1] the score this year is 7.11; next year it could be 8.2 or 8.3 from my monitoring of the system as it's running at present. That's an enormous jump and why? Because we have established a secure place for youngsters. They will ask you now, 'Please sir, hear me read.' The kids are now keen readers, they are anxious to read to you, even for ten minutes. This school has an SPA intake, even though we don't get the allowance; 7.6 is the median for the whole of the authority and we have 7.11 with an SPA intake.

Though fully aware of the need to win support for his views from the rest of his staff, Mr Riley felt that teachers owed parents more both in terms of time and respect, than they generally received:

Teachers need to come down from the pedestal that they've been on for years; they've got a superior attitude about themselves. Alright, there's certain things that they are scared about; some teachers are inadequate so they build protection around themselves and the best way to remain secure is to keep parents at a distance. They must have time for people; they must have time for parents; they must come down off their pedestal and treat people as human beings and they must acknowledge that other people have an identity and other people need respect. We don't need much boosting in our job; it's a very fulfilling job, teaching. You've got raw materials and here you are, turning out beautiful pieces of sculpture. But lots of people have a hum-drum job, terrible jobs and we're the privileged few, so why stand on pedestals? We must motivate them, and above all, must let the children see that we respect their parents.

The teachers at St Hilda's had a very similar view of parental involvement to their headmaster and there was no sign of friction between them. In fact the deputy head, Mr Reid, thought parents should be more involved on the educational side of the school than at present:

---

[1] i.e. The year of the case study.

When we talk about parent-and-teacher associations my experience has been that there is rather too much on the social side and not enough on the educational side. There ought to be more parental involvement in what the school is trying to do and we should be trying to get the parents to see what the school is doing to help their child.

Opinions of the parents' main role *vis-à-vis* the school varied according to the age of the children in each teacher's class. Mr Ronan, who taught a class of ten-year-olds, felt that parents should support the school financially and back up the teacher in what he or she did.

On the other hand, Mrs Roper, with a class of four- and five-year-olds, thought that the parents' main role should be to discipline their children at home and help them with their social behaviour including toilet training, use of knife and fork, and how to dress themselves. They should also hear their children read as often as possible when they first started. She felt that the children needed to read at home with their parents otherwise they did not make any progress. Parents who read to their children at home had more effect on their reading standards than her tuition.

Opinions about parents working in the classroom varied. Paradoxically, it was in the nursery that they were least encouraged. Though parents were welcome to come in if they had problems with their children, difficulties arose, explained the nursery staff, if they stayed to help. Mrs Russell, the NNEB helper, thought few parents realized the purpose of a nursery but tended to treat it like a playgroup. If parents stayed on to help after bringing their children in the morning they tended to treat the children like babies, probably due to their lack of experience or training. Mrs O'Rourke, the nursery teacher, agreed, adding that she would not have a parent helping whose own child was in the nursery.

The two infant teachers were happier about parents helping in the classroom, though they were divided on the question of letting them hear children read. Mrs Roper said she liked to choose which parents came in, preferring someone who would enjoy working with the children but who did not have her own child in the class.

If they are used in a supporting role, then they may have qualities that the teacher doesn't have. For example, I'm very poor on the girls' art and craft side; it would help if parents came in and did sewing and that type of thing with the girls.

The views of the teachers at Spiritus Sanctus echoed those of their headmaster for the most part. Suspicion of parents extended to suspicion of educational researchers and only one teacher at the school agreed to his interview being tape-recorded.

In general it was hoped that parents would support the school. As with St Hilda's, the form this support should take varied according to the age of the children taught. The nursery and infant staff emphasized the need for children to be toilet-trained before they came to school in addition to being able to dress themselves and to use a knife and fork properly. The nursery teacher, Mrs Jacobs, added that parents should encourage their children to trust their teachers and confide in them if they needed help. Two of the junior teachers mentioned a need for increased parental discipline; the school should not be held responsible for children's late bedtimes. The deputy-head, Mr Jones, who had 10 children of his own, expected parents to show the same interest in their children as he in his:

> I think my duty as a parent has been to back up the teachers in the work they have been trying to do. I made it a point that whenever anything was going on at school to which parents were invited, I was there, and I made sure that they knew I was interested. The teachers knew me and I knew them and the children knew that both teachers and parents knew them.

Teachers at Spiritus Sanctus were generally against the idea of parents helping in classroom activities, though two or three suggested that they might help with art and craft, preferably *outside* the classroom. Mr James, a junior teacher, felt that if one parent was allowed to help in the classroom, they would all want to come in and some parents just were not suitable, they were not capable of dealing with children. Mrs Cleeve, one of the two infant teachers, agreed, adding that even when they accompanied the children on school trips, some parents could be more trouble than they were worth. The major drawback to their involvement in classroom activities was their complete lack of training. Even when helping with cookery, parents did not realize that it was the *process* of making a cake that mattered, together with the concomitant possibilities for language development and number work, as well as the quality of the cake itself. Mrs Griffin, the second infant teacher, also raised the problem of parents' bias towards their own child. If a parent helped in the same class as her own child, she maintained, she could never treat it in the same manner as the rest

Parents might also hear children read, though reservations were expressed concerning the need for confidentiality:

> Sometimes, if you are not careful, there can be criticisms or comments dropped to other parents; if this is done in the wrong context there could be trouble.

Mr Reid was convinced of the use that *could* be made of parents in reading:

> In my view, young children need someone to read to, they need an audience. If they have an adult to read to, this, I find, stimulates them to reading, it encourages better effort. Also, where a child will only read on its own for 15 minutes or so unaided, it will read for a longer period without tiring or losing concentration if it has a grown-up to read to.

As in the other case-study schools, teachers were divided on the question of counselling parents. Many of the younger ones felt they were not qualified to advise parents on anything other than the education of their children. One teacher commented that parents just would not come to her for advice because she was a lot younger and less experienced than they were. Even those teachers whom parents did approach stressed that the help they could provide was necessarily limited. Mr Ronan said the type of advice he would feel qualified to give depended on the type of problem presented to him:

> On some things I would be prepared to say, 'Do this,' or 'Do that,' whereas, if they came with a highly personal problem where the wrong advice might split up a marriage, I would fight shy of saying anything. I think if it was that type of problem one would have to have special qualifications to deal with it; special training.

Mr Reid also regarded his experience as limited, even though he himself was a grandfather and approaching retirement.

> I think it can be very dangerous if you're not careful, you can get involved in something that is beyond your experience. I am not a marriage guidance counsellor and I think that often the wise thing to do is to pass parents on to a more experienced agency.

The main problem teachers foresaw in having parental help in the classroom concerned the mother who might try to criticize or take over from the teacher. One of the infant teachers said that during a PE lesson a mother had criticized her for allowing her child to go to the top of the climbing frame, though the teacher knew that he was quite capable of doing so safely. Another, and perhaps more serious problem, was raised by Miss Raven, a newly-qualified junior teacher:

> I had a difficult parent during my last parents' evening. I was accused of picking on her child, so it was my word against the child's word, which wasn't very nice. The child was an angel at home and she (the mother) couldn't see how he could be any different at school. In the end she came to see Mr Riley and he backed me up because he knew the child in question. It boiled down to the fact that I had caught this child cheating a few times and he did not like it. So rather than wait for me to say to the mother that I had caught him cheating, he told her first that I was picking on him.

However, in spite of these problems and all their other reservations, the teaching staff at St Hilda's were unanimously in favour of involving parents in their children's education. One junior teacher justified it as follows:

> The children get enormous pleasure from being able to bring their mother in to show what they are doing. I think when a parent knows what's going on and knows that they are welcome in the school, it's good for the child; they take more trouble in their work when they know their parents are interested in what they are doing. I've found in the two or three years since we have been involving parents that children are much more ready when they leave in the afternoon to drag their parents back into the class-room to show them the work they've been doing. If they want to show their mothers the work they've done, then they want to show them something good; it's a sense of achievement in their work that prompts them to bring their mothers in.

Thus, in St Hilda's both the head and most of his staff were enthusi-astic about involving parents in the life of the school, while at the same time being fully aware of the problems to which this could give rise. Their willingness to recognize these problems and face up to them added to the sense of commitment to parental involvement as perceived by the visiting project team.

Spiritus Sanctus Primary

The atmosphere at Spiritus Sanctus was markedly different from that at St Hilda's. Relationships between teachers and children appeared much more restrained (for instance the staff had their own table in the hall, separate from the children, at lunchtime). The curriculum was fairly structured even in the infants' department, with basic language and number work done in the morning and any art and craft left to the afternoon. The teaching approach was class based and teacher centred with little group work in evidence. A gold and silver star system for good work was in operation in the junior classes and there was keen competition between these four classes for the highest weekly attendance figures.

Following the team's first visit to the school a few of the teachers became deeply suspicious of the motives for carrying out the research and in particular for observing them in their classrooms. Much reassurance was needed before the research was allowed to continue.

Mr Ryan, the headmaster, was married with three children and had been teaching for over 30 years. He had been head of Spiritus Sanctus for 10 of those years. His attitude to parents was a great deal more guarded than that of Mr Riley. He saw their main role very much as supportive of the school, but was also concerned that they should do their best to ensure their child's happiness when he or she first started attending:

> Before they start school parents should talk to their children about going to school as if it were something attractive, something to which they should look forward. They should tell them that everyone will be looking after them and that they will see them at school occasionally and that if there were anything wrong they could come and see their teacher. They should treat it as if the child were going to stay with its aunty for a week or two; not sentimentally or emotionally but as if it were staying with its aunty.

However, he drew a line between social education, which was the home's responsibility, and cognitive education, which was that of the school:

> I would rather parents didn't attempt to teach children formally before they come to school because they invariably do it wrong, they teach in a different way to us. For instance, when they teach them their letters, they teach them to print capitals instead of lower case letters. They teach them the 'ordinary' alphabet and not the 'phonic' alphabet and I always tell parents that if they read to their children and have their children on their knee while they are doing it so that they can look at the book, this is far

better. We do also expect that by the time they come to school, they can fasten their own buttons and see to themselves going to the lavatory and that sort of thing.

He was definitely against parents helping in the classroom, feeling that any help must necessarily constitute teaching, something which they had not been trained to do. He continued:

Even if you say that they can come in and do the mechanical jobs like cutting up paper, they don't do it, even then, to the satisfaction of the teacher. They don't realize that if a teacher asks for pieces of paper 4 inches square, they mean corners of 90 degrees. I can see a use for a specific parent; for instance Mrs-so-and-so might be very good at embroidery and you could ask her to come in and show the top class girls a few stitches. Now I know that that woman is teaching, but at least she is an expert in her field. I don't think you can bring any parent or all parents in indiscriminately.

There was also another difficulty associated with parents helping:

Even if we had a parent who was a trained and experienced teacher it would take some time for that newcomer to pick up the ways and methods of the teacher taking that class. This seems to be the main difficulty, that you have to spend so much time getting your helper to do things in the way that you want. What may have worked for that parent when she was teaching may not suit Mrs Smith in this class or Mrs Jones in that.

The school did, however, have a Parents' Association, though accord-ing to Mr Ryan its sole concern was the raising of money and the promoting of social events. He did not have a very high opinion of the Association and its committee.

When it comes to doing anything we, that is the staff, have to do most of the work. We can do it much more efficiently and much more quickly with much less effort if we are just allowed to get on with it, instead of making it look as though they are doing it.

As far as counselling parents with problems was concerned Mr Ryan's approach was pragmatic:

I don't think it should be part of my job but it is. This is a poorish area and there is a large number of parents who can't cope in one way or another and hardly a week goes by without some parent coming in who needs help. They've got to the far end and wherever they turn they are not able to get the help that they want. Here I should mention, perhaps, that the deputy head is a Samaritan of long experience, with a large family of his own who are now growing up, and is an excellent person for this sort of thing. So when a specific form of help is required, such as information on what agencies are available, where to go, who to see, then very often I ask him to come and see the parent concerned.

Mr Ryan was quite conscious that he painted a picture of himself as being antagonistic to parents. He felt that in many ways he had been forced into this position:

I somehow feel that I've given the impression I would like a big notice over the door saying, 'No parents beyond this point', and it isn't like that at all. But from talking to many other head teachers it seems that we are almost forced into the position of putting up a notice like this, because if we didn't, we just wouldn't be able to run the school. When I opened this school the idea was that the gates and doors were left wide open. But very soon we had to make some rules and we keep to them because if we ever relax and let parents come in, then the abuses start. Their toddlers are racing up and down the corridor and climbing over the rail to the cloakroom; we even have to have a notice up in the infants' corridor saying 'No smoking'. Parents come and stare through the classroom door and make signs to their children. They even open the classroom door and walk in to their child at the back of the class and say, 'You've forgotten your lunch, love.' So unfortunately, from time to time we have to put our foot down and make sure that parents don't overstep the mark.

He justified the stance he took by telling us it was his experience that parents just did not *want* to be involved in school, they were not concerned about how their child was taught so long as the level of education was up to their expectations.

The majority of parents in my experience are not very concerned about their children's progress as long as they are reading as well as the children that come in and play with them, and as long as their writing and spelling is reasonable. The complaints that we get, such as they are, are that the children are being upset by being pressed, not that they are falling behind by not being pressed. This is what parents complain about; not that Johnny *can't* do long division but that he's been *made* to do long division.

The views of the teachers at Spiritus Sanctus echoed those of their headmaster for the most part. Suspicion of parents extended to suspicion of educational researchers and only one teacher at the school agreed to his interview being tape-recorded.

In general it was hoped that parents would support the school. As with St Hilda's, the form this support should take varied according to the age of the children taught. The nursery and infant staff emphasized the need for children to be toilet-trained before they came to school in addition to being able to dress themselves and to use a knife and fork properly. The nursery teacher, Mrs Jacobs, added that parents should encourage their children to trust their teachers and confide in them if they needed help. Two of the junior teachers mentioned a need for increased parental discipline; the school should not be held responsible for children's late bedtimes. The deputy-head, Mr Jones, who had 10 children of his own, expected parents to show the same interest in their children as he in his:

> I think my duty as a parent has been to back up the teachers in the work they have been trying to do. I made it a point that whenever anything was going on at school to which parents were invited, I was there, and I made sure that they knew I was interested. The teachers knew me and I knew them and the children knew that both teachers and parents knew them.

Teachers at Spiritus Sanctus were generally against the idea of parents helping in classroom activities, though two or three suggested that they might help with art and craft, preferably *outside* the classroom. Mr James, a junior teacher, felt that if one parent was allowed to help in the classroom, they would all want to come in and some parents just were not suitable, they were not capable of dealing with children. Mrs Cleeve, one of the two infant teachers, agreed, adding that even when they accompanied the children on school trips, some parents could be more trouble than they were worth. The major drawback to their involvement in classroom activities was their complete lack of training. Even when helping with cookery, parents did not realize that it was the *process* of making a cake that mattered, together with the concomitant possibilities for language development and number work, as well as the quality of the cake itself. Mrs Griffin, the second infant teacher, also raised the problem of parents' bias towards their own child. If a parent helped in the same class as her own child, she maintained, she could never treat it in the same manner as the rest of the class; a parent could never be impartial. Mr Jones agreed, giving a dramatic example of what could happen if an over-anxious parent helped in the same class as her child:

> I can see problems arising if parents work in classrooms, one being a parent who becomes very jealous because her child isn't achieving as much success in reading as other children are. I heard about a case like this where the mother concerned lost her temper with her child and gave the child a good smacking in front of the teacher and the rest of the class! This seems to me to be a deplorable state of affairs! I know that might be an extreme case, but I can still see the possibility of these petty jealousies and hatreds growing up. I think a parent would be too involved with the well-being of her own child in that class, unlike the teacher whose care has to encompass all of them.

However, Mr Jones was happier than his colleagues about asking for parents' help with activities outside the classroom:

> I've found parents invaluable when we've gone on school trips to the local zoo, where we've been forced to break up into small groups to take the children round. We didn't have enough staff but lots of the mothers volunteered and said that they would come if we wanted them, and they came along and it was ideal. They each took charge of a little group and went round and we met at certain times for lunch and refreshments. Each group had about eight or nine children and it was just right.

A different view was taken by Mrs Stabley, the nursery helper, who felt that though parents might be useful on school visits, there was always the possibility of the 'wrong' sort of parent coming. She gave an account of a visit the nursery had made to the same zoo, for which parental help had been recruited:

> The children were split into groups with five children to one adult. They were told they should not bring any money for sweets on the bus for fear of them being sick. One mother who came to help was continually going over to her own child, who had not been assigned to the group in her charge, seeing that she was alright and making sure she noticed all the things in the zoo. Towards the end of the visit, this child repeatedly asked for an ice-lolly in spite of the fact that we had told all the children they couldn't have one. As we got on the bus to come home, the child's mother disappeared, holding up the bus. She reappeared

with a box full of ice-lollies, bought out of her own money, one for each of the children. We were annoyed at this, especially as she was one ice-lolly short and had to go back and queue again, thus making us even later on our return.

The teachers at Spiritus Sanctus were divided on the question of counselling parents. Two or three felt that parents did not come to them for advice as they were too young. The infant staff said that they gave advice when parents requested it but felt it would be inappropriate to do so where the problem did not directly affect the child.

Finally, none of the teachers thought that parents had any real idea of the aims of the curriculum and the teaching methods in use. One of the junior teachers complained:

> Parents think the whole point of the school is to teach the 3Rs; they don't realize the variety of things that go on in a modern classroom.

The nursery staff agreed, adding that parents often needed to be told what the nursery was trying to do. They sometimes regarded it merely as a child-minding service. However, Mr Jones wondered whether parents really needed to know anything about teaching methods:

> I don't really know whether it's necessary for them to understand methods; if the aims are good and high enough, I don't see that they need to understand methods. After all, I don't understand the methods they use in their various types of employment, but if the end result is good, then I acclaim them for what they are doing.

The extent to which parents do need to be informed of the teaching methods in use in their children's school is a matter of current debate (e.g. Taylor Report, DES 1977). However, the attitude which engendered this opinion may be seen as indicative of the general view of parents as, at best, amateurs in a world of professionals. The unwillingness of both head and teaching staff to allow these amateurs into the classroom, or even into the school, contrasted strikingly with the approach adopted by the staff at St Hilda's to what was essentially a very similar body of parents. It was to these parents the project team turned in an effort to discern the differential effect on them of these two contrasting approaches.

The Parents

Parents at both schools were selected for interview in a similar manner to those at the other case study schools (i.e. every tenth name from the school registers). As before, any oversampling was compensated for by those parents whom, for one reason or another, it was not possible to contact in the time available. Interviews were conducted in parents' homes, and they appeared generally very welcoming after any initial suspicions had been overcome. In the majority of cases a tape-recorder was not used as for much of the time the interviewer had to compete for parents' attention with young children or the TV set, or occasionally both. All parents professed a concern for their children's education and often spent some time in making this clear.

Surprisingly enough, bearing in mind the contrasting approaches to parental involvement taken by the two schools, the views of both sets of parents were remarkably similar in content, though different in spirit. Mr Ryan, the head of Spiritus Sanctus, appeared perfectly justified in his claim that parents were not greatly concerned about teaching methods. Certainly, the large majority of parents interviewed seemed happy to 'leave it to the professionals' for the most part, and there was little or no criticism of curriculum or method; parents felt that the experts knew best. Most of the parents had only a vague idea of what their children did at school all day. One mother described her children's school day thus:

> It's mostly English and reading Lee does, I think; that's all he talks about, his reading. Donna talks about her reading as well. She tells me about the books she had and the book she's gone on to, and if she's nearly come to the end of a book.' (Mother of two, Spiritus Sanctus.)

In fact Lee was in the second year of the juniors and Donna in the second year of the infants. From observation in the respective classrooms it was apparent that the curriculum was *far* wider and more varied than this mother supposed.

The majority of both sets of parents had chosen a Catholic school for their children as they were Catholic themselves (father or mother or both) and wished them to be educated in the faith. A significant minority, however, said that the school had been selected because it was close at hand, or because it had a good reputation. Generally, parents were glad that religion was not 'pushed down your throat like when we were at school'. One parent commented: 'They don't pump you with religion like they used to.'

However, four parents also commented on the apparent lack of interest on the part of the parish priest, complaining that he was not spending enough time at the school to give the children a proper grounding in the Catholic faith. This apparent lack of interest was perhaps unfortunate in that a strong link between the schools and the local churches might well have served as another basis for contact between home and school, the improvement of which was the avowed aim of at least one of these schools.

The main thing parents wanted school to give their children was 'a good education' though few were able to explain what their idea of a good education was. Many thought of it as preparing the children for secondary school, 'where the real learning took place'. The nursery was seen as providing companionship, teaching children to mix with others of their own age. It also broadened the children's experience and prepared them for infant school. Few attributed any educational objectives to nursery education.

The most important curricular subjects were usually thought to be the 3 Rs with most stress laid on reading. However, a number of parents felt that their children were receiving a far better education than they themselves had been given, and, as Mr Riley claimed, parents were generally concerned that their children should be happy at school:

> The school should teach them properly. I don't want the children frightened, like we were at school, when if you couldn't get it right the teacher would come and knock you on the head; that makes you work less. Our kids are quite bright; they're not brilliant but they're doing very well, and that's because there's an easier atmosphere at the school. (Mother of seven, St Hilda's.)

Many parents from St Hilda's were reasonably satisifed that they knew enough about their children's day at school, though in general those with children at Spiritus Sanctus were a little more curious. Parents from both schools expressed an anxiety about 'interfering' or 'taking up too much of the teachers' time'. Parents from Spiritus Sanctus did not always find the staff approachable:

> Some of them are alright. Mr Ryan, he seems to be a nice enough fellow; but sometimes you get the impression that they don't want to know; they're just there to teach your children; they've got no real time for you. (Mother of two, Spiritus Sanctus.)

Parents from St Hilda's, in contrast, stressed the welcoming nature of the staff and the ease of access to the school if they had anything they wished to discuss:

> I think being open to parents makes the children feel more secure, my children are definitely not frightened of Mr Riley or of their teachers. (Mother of two, St Hilda's.)

There were mixed feelings on the question of helping in school. Many parents from both schools explained that, although they might be interested in helping, lack of time made it impossible, either because they had a young child still at home or a job:

> I enjoy being with the children but the only thing is, since I've got this job, I've found it might be a bit too much really. It's very hectic when you've got two children and a job. (Mother of two, St Hilda's.)

A substantial minority felt that parents should not be asked to help in school, teaching being best left to the teachers. A parent with two children at St Hilda's explained her misgivings:

> We don't agree with parents helping with the education part; that should be left to people who are qualified. The thing is this: I don't think Mr Riley's aware of it, but some of the parents who are helping, listening to children read, are gossips. They're getting their heads together and gossiping about our children and I don't think that's fair, I don't think children should be scandalized in that way. I've been behind people going to school and heard them talking. I don't believe in that; I don't think parents should go in and hear other people's children read.

It was generally felt that the chance to meet and talk to other parents was useful. Many of those interviewed had met other parents while taking their children to school or collecting them in the afternoon. Both schools had parents' associations and attitudes to them varied. Three or four parents from St Hilda's commented that their association was run by a few mothers only, 'a chosen few' as one of them described it. However, other parents were quite happy with this oligarchy!

> We have a parent-teacher association there (St Hilda's) and they've done marvellous things with the money collected.

> They've got little reading centres outside practically every class-
> room where the kids can go with headphones and everything.
> It's not a committee thing, the PTA, all parents are free to join in,
> but some have more time than we have, and they're on it most of
> the time. But we don't say that they are the ones who are pushy;
> they are doing great things for the school. You've got to have
> someone who'll do the organizing, haven't you?

The real difference the project team discerned between the attitudes
of parents to each school has already been touched upon in discussion
of the approachability and accessibility of the teachers. This difference
expressed itself in the spirit rather than the content of the interviews
conducted and can best be explained in terms of the 'active' satisfaction
of St Hilda's parents compared with the 'passive' satisfaction of those
from Spiritus Sanctus. The enthusiasm expressed by parents for St
Hilda's was not matched by a similar attitude to Spiritus Sanctus, many
of whose parents were content to leave teaching to the teachers as long
as their children appeared to them 'to be getting on alright' and brought
no problems home.

Though it is impossible to measure attitude change between groups
without recourse to a more objective form of measurement than the
semi-structured interview, the project team were forced to the conclusion that the similarities between the educational viewpoints of each
school's parents far outweighed the differences. If this is true, then the
unavoidable implication is that parental attitudes to education are
influenced very little by attempts to involve them in the activities of
their children's school. Whatever the claims made by Mr Riley concerning the improved reading standards of his pupils following his opening
of the school to parents, the project team found little to justify any
assumption that increased parental involvement led to a change in
parental attitude to schools and thus to improved pupil attainment.
What they found far more significant was that, whereas less than half
the parents interviewed claimed to have enjoyed their own school days,
they almost without exception said that their children loved going, this
being equally as true for Spiritus Sanctus as for St Hilda's. If a happy
child works harder and attains more than an unhappy one, which some
educational theorists would have us believe, then this may weigh considerably more heavily in the long run than these parents' lack of
knowledge of (or interest in) their children's school curriculum and the
methods used to instruct them. It is perhaps concern for the happiness
of the pupils in their charge that is the decisive factor separating the

two heads. Mr Riley, realizing that parents wish their children to be happy at school ('Regardless of how many skills they pick up, it is happiness that is number one'), may in the long run achieve far more in influencing parents' attitudes than Mr Ryan in his dismissive account of parents coming in to complain that 'their children have nightmares and are crying all night because they don't want to come to school'.

It is, of course, impossible to estimate the implications (if any) of the differing approaches of these two schools for the education, both social and cognitive, of their pupils, and the apparent similarity in educational viewpoints between the two sets of parents may be due to the fact that three years is too short a time for Mr Riley to have made a significant impression on the attitudes of the parents at his school.

Chapter 10

Summing Up

With the publication of the Plowden Report in 1967 (DES), the significance of the part which parents have to play in the education of their children was for the first time given official recognition and endorsement. A minimum programme for all primary schools was recommended which included the welcoming of parents into school, regular meetings between teachers and parents, and the sending of written information to parents about their children's progress and the school's activities on a regular basis.

It was suggested that various benefits to the children might ensue from the closer links thus developed between home and school. In fact, little evidence existed for this supposition at that time (the middle 1960s) nor has conclusive evidence emerged as a result of the various initiatives in this field of endeavour since that time. This issue was reviewed at some length in Chapter 1. There remains, however, a common conviction amongst educationists that the involvement of parents in their children's education can only be beneficial, although the forms which this involvement should take are not generally agreed. This conviction has been complemented in recent times by the emergence of parent-pressure groups (e.g. those involved in the Campaign for the Advancement of State Education (CASE), and those responsible for the Parents' Charter).

It was against this background of increasing interest at least on the part of some parents and the convictions of educationists that the present study was undertaken. Its purpose was to investigate the extent to which parents are currently being involved in their children's primary education, and the various means which schools are adopting to bring this about.

Evaluation of the different forms and incidence of such involvement was not its object. The project brief was to conduct a national sample survey of primary schools, complemented by case study material of a qualitative nature. The development of a questionnaire, and its use with a national random sample of primary schools in England and Wales is described in detail in Chapter 2.

The questionnaire was addressed to head-teachers, and the data it yielded were therefore based upon their perceptions; these are reported in Chapter 3. About one-third of primary schools now have a formal PTA. A further quarter have an informal, 'Friends of the School', organization which serves a similar purpose. This constitutes a significant increase over the last decade. In relation to the minimum programme recommended in Plowden, the data suggest that the other 'traditional' forms of contact between home and school, parents' evenings and open days, occur in over 95 per cent of primary schools, with an attendance level of over three-quarters of parents in half of these. Such 'formal' contacts between parents and teachers are supplemented in over 90 per cent of schools by contact of a more informal nature. Sixty-five per cent of schools send written information about themselves to new parents, with 92 per cent inviting new parents to visit them before their children start to attend. In marked contrast, less than half of all primary schools send written reports concerning children's work and/or behaviour to parents, those doing so being predominantly the schools for older children (i.e. 7 to 13 years). Home visiting is carried out as a matter of policy in connection with about half of all primary schools by education welfare officers or home liaison workers of various kinds. In 22 per cent of schools, predominantly nurseries and schools with nursery classes, such home visiting is undertaken by the head or assistant teachers.

The wide variety of ways in which schools attempt to involve parents is complemented by a variety of associated problems. It is perhaps hardly surprising that parental apathy, reluctance to become involved, looms largest amongst these. Bearing this in mind, the views of the 55 per cent of heads reporting an increase in parental involvement over the past two years may be optimistic, as might also those of the 65 per cent reporting a change in parental attitude as a consequence of this increased involvement.

The relationship between schools and their pupils' parents changes with the age of the children. There was evidence in the case studies which suggests that parents feel progressively less competent in relation to the school curriculum as their children grow older. Ann Garvey (1977) also reported this. Two broad types of parental involvement seem to exist, one adopted by schools catering mainly for children of less than eight years of age, the other by schools catering for older children. The way in which the different aspects of parental involvement characterize these two types is reported in Chapter 4. A 'social service' role played by schools in advising parents on social and domestic problems was revealed in the survey and explored more fully in the case studies. It is in this aspect of the parent/school relationship that nursery schools and classes assume real importance, with over 90 per cent of nursery schools engaging in this practice. An interesting corollary to this new educational role is that higher levels of school based involvement are consistently reported by head teachers who also attribute some of their pupils' in-school behaviour problems to home circumstances. A possible inference is that those heads conscious of the difficulties their pupils face at home are more willing to involve parents in school, using this involvement therapeutically for the parents as well as educationally for the children. The implications that this change in role may have for the teaching profession are set out and discussed in Chapter 7.

The willingness of parents to become involved in school activities, and of the school to woo its parents, is hedged about by a number of constraints. Of these the chief appears to be the social class of the parents (in spite of the urgings of Plowden and the 'witness' of the Plowden-recommended Educational Priority Areas). Almost equal in importance as measured by the number of different types of involvement it influences, is staff—pupil ratio, to which it is inversely related. School design (architecture) and the way the curriculum is organized, also have a strong influence; schools featuring 'open', as opposed to closed-box, classroom design and an integrated curriculum manifesting significantly higher levels of school and classroom based parental involvement. School size also influences parental involvement, the larger schools attracting more. The period of the present head-teacher's incumbency, rate of staff turnover and rate of pupil turnover influence parental involvement in a curvilinear manner; the prevalence of various types of involvement increases as 'school stability' (as measured by these factors) decreases, up to a point, beyond which it increases again. Clearly schools need a measure of change but cannot cope with too much. Neither pupils' ethnic origins nor the prevalence of working mothers in a school seemed to exert much influence. These are all discussed in detail in Chapter 5, as is the influence of LEA policy.

The case studies provide an interesting counterpoint to the theme of parental involvement which emerges from the survey. The views of assistant teachers are presented and discussed in Chapter 7, and those of parents in Chapter 8. Since the parents interviewed were selected at random, the perspective of the non-involved majority are included. It must be recalled, however, that only 10 schools were selected for intensive study and the conclusions, though plausible, must be treated with caution. The majority of parents expressed satisfaction with the schools' endeavours on behalf of their children, a satisfaction, however, based apparently upon scanty knowledge of what actually went on in the schools. In spite of the efforts made to inform them and to involve them (described in detail in Chapter 8), for the most part they neither wished, nor felt the need to be involved in their children's school lives. Underlying this 'laissez faire' attitude, feelings of inadequacy in the face of the 'professional' could often be discerned.

For their part, the teachers were in reality anxious to defend the professional integrity of their role from the wholesale intrusion of 'parental amateurs', and worried that the demands made on their time by those parents seeking 'counselling' impinged unjustifiably on their proper task, the education of the children.

Despite parental reluctance and teacher misgiving, parental involvement, taking various forms, flourished in all the case study schools, and seems generally to be on the increase (p. 50). The most recent official pronouncement reiterates its positive values.

> It is the individual parent who is in law responsible for securing his child's education and whose support in this task is vital. There should therefore be at the individual level also a partnership between home and school. The individual parent will want the school to be an open and welcoming place. He will expect it to provide a framework within which he can communicate with his own child's teachers, in a spirit of partnership, about the child's welfare and progress.

> We believe that such aspirations are wholly reasonable and that every parent has a right to expect a school's teachers to recognise his status in the education of his child by the practical arrangements they make to communicate with him and the spirit in which they accept his interest. If there is no such recognition, the measures we have advocated for parents collectively will be of limited value, and may be seen by many parents and teachers as no more than a means of increasing the influence of those who

are already enthusiastic participators. We wish to produce a structure within which every parent will have a role in supporting the school and increasing its effectiveness.' (*A New Partnership for Our Schools*, DES, 1977, 5:26, 27).

What remains an open question, of course, is the potential benefit in terms of children's school attainments. The 'syllogism of parental participation' proposed by Young and McGeeney (1968):

A rise in the level of parental encouragement augments their children's performance at school.

Teachers by involving parents in the school bring about a rise in the level of parental encouragement.

Teachers by involving parents in the school augment the children's performance.

remains largely unproven. As was earlier pointed out, it was not the purpose of this study to gather evidence which might have resolved the matter. What is evident from this study is that the involvement of parents to any significant degree in the life of their children's school is no easy matter. It is hindered by a lack of enthusiasm on the part of many, mainly working class, parents, and by many inherent features of schools. For their part teachers rightly perceive parents as an additional and avoidable complication in an already demanding professional life. They also fear that the broadening of their professional role evident in recent times, of which the 'counselling' of parents is an example, may lead to its dilution, with their energies expended in a variety of ways peripheral and debilitating to their main task, educating children. Further, young teachers, whilst expressing a willingness to involve parents in school life and thus to become involved more deeply in the family lives of their pupils, express feelings of inadequacy by reason of their own youth and inexperience. In common with their more mature colleagues they also point to the lack in their initial training of any preparation for this wider and more demanding role.

Parental involvement in primary schools is a topic, amongst many others in education, in respect of which teachers are under pressure to make fairly radical changes in their ways of working, in the hope, rather than the certainty, that the outcome will justify the effort. The survey data suggest that primary schools have progressed cautiously towards a greater involvement of parents over the decade since Plowden; the case studies suggest reasons why the progress has been, and should continue to be, cautious.

APPENDICES

Appendix (i) The Questionnaire

NAME OF SCHOOL: . . . .

D.E.S. No. ☐☐☐☐☐☐☐

NAME OF HEAD: . . . .

L.E.A.: . . . .

This questionnaire is part of a national survey of parental involvement in the primary school. It was developed in consultation with a large number of head-teachers of primary schools throughout England and Wales and with the help and advice of teacher unions, parent organizations and other interested bodies.

As one of the schools selected in the random sample, your cooperation in the completion and early return of this questionnaire would be very much appreciated.

Please answer this questionnaire by circling numbers or words, or ticking boxes as appropriate. Please ignore the boxes at the right-hand side of the page (these are for office use only).

To avoid any misunderstanding, it would be helpful if you would read this questionnaire through once before completing it.

1. Type of School

	1−7

Nursery school   1
Infant or First school with nursery unit   2
Infant or First school without nursery unit   3
JMI or Combined with nursery unit   4   □ 8
JMI or Combined without nursery unit   5
Junior or Middle school   6

2. School Size

N.B. Part-time pupils should be counted as full-time.

(a) Under 50 pupils on roll   1
     51–100 pupils on roll   2
     101–150 pupils on roll   3
     151–250 pupils on roll   4   □ 9
     251–350 pupils on roll   5_
     351–500 pupils on roll   6

(b) *Staff/pupil ratio*
     Please tick one box for each department, as appropriate
     to your school.

*One member of staff to:	*Nursery*	*Infant or First*	*Junior or Middle*
1 Under 10 pupils			
2 10–15 pupils			
3 16–20 pupils			
4 31–30 pupils			
5 31–35 pupils			
6 36–40 pupils			
7 over 41 pupils			
	□ 10	□ 11	□ 12

* 'A member of staff' includes teachers, welfare assistants other
than school meals assistants), NNEB trained assistants, as well as
the head.

(c) *School staffing*
Please indicate the number of staff in your school in each of the
following categories.

   (i) Full-time teachers
      (including head and deputy-head)   ☐ ☐ 13

  (ii) Part-time teachers   ☐ ☐ 14

  (iii) Please indicate to how many full-time teachers (ii) is
      equivalent   ☐ ☐ 15

  (iv) Welfare and unqualified nursery assistants
      (other than school meals assistants)   ☐ ☐ 16

  (v) NNEB trained assistants   ☐ ☐ 17

  (vi) Other – please specify   ☐ ☐ 18

. . . .

. . . .

(d) Has your school been designated a social priority school   YES
under the terms of the Burnham agreement or as being of   NO ☐ 19
special educational difficulty?

(e) Is your school taking part in any community development   YES
project initiated or organized by the local authority?   NO ☐ 20

If yes, is the school allocated any additional resources?   YES
  NO ☐ 21

If yes, please indicate the nature of the resources:

   (i) Building (e.g. community hall attached to school)   YES
      NO ☐ 22

  (ii) Staff (e.g. community worker attached to, or   YES
      working in association with the school)   NO ☐ 23

  (iii) Financial (e.g. grant by local authority towards   YES
      purchase of school equipment)   NO ☐ 24

  (iv) Other – please specify

. . . .

. . . .

3. School Age

(a) Was your school built:

before 1900	1
1900–1920	2
1921–1930	3
1931–1950	4
1951–1960	5
1961–1970	6
1971 or after	7

☐ 25

(b) Has the initial school building been added to at any time or substantially altered?

YES
NO   ☐ 26

If yes, please give details:

☐☐☐☐ 27–30

. . . .

. . . .

. . . .

4. School Architecture

Which of the following best describes the way in which your school is designed? Would you please circle the number(s) in the appropriate category(ies).

	Nursery	*Infant or First*	*Junior or Middle*
Traditional school. Classroom type design with no hall, or with hall separate from main school building	1	1	1
Traditional, classroom-type design; no room available other than hall for group or communal activities	2	2	2
As above but some space available for integrated or small-group activities	3	3	3
Design partially open-plan, with some classroom units	4	4	4
Design totally open-plan, with or without partitions which may be drawn across to create classroom units	5	5	5
	□ 31	□ 32	□ 33

5. Organization

Which of the following *best* describes the teaching approach in your school? Would you please circle the number(s) in the appropriate category(ies).

	Nursery	*Infant or First*	*Junior or Middle*
Unstreamed classes, totally or partially vertically-grouped; staff organized into units for team-teaching and an integrated day approach	1	1	1
Unstreamed classes, totally or partially vertically-grouped; class rather than team-teaching with an integrated day approach	2	2	2
As above but with traditional organization (e.g. basic subjects am and creative activities pm)	3	3	3
Unstreamed classes, horizontally grouped; team or cooperative teaching with an integrated day approached	4	4	4
Unstreamed classes, horizontally grouped; class rather than team-teaching with an integrated day approach	5	5	5
Unstreamed classes, horizontally grouped, generally taught by one person with a structured curriculum	6	6	6
As above but classes streamed or setted for some or all subjects	7	7	7
	☐ 34	☐ 35	☐ 36

6. School Location

(a) Which of the following *best* describes the area in which the children at your school live? (*Please circle only one category.*)

Houses are closely packed together with many in a poor state of repair and with some multi-occupation	1
An area of council housing characterized by high-rise flats	2
An area dominated by a large council estate	3
An area of mixed council and privately owned housing of the less expensive type	4
An urban/suburban area of mostly private housing	5
A suburban private housing estate with large, detached or semi-detached houses	6
A rural or semi-rural area	7
An area of mixed housing covering two or more of the above categories	8

☐ 37

(b) Is your school intake governed or modified by a connection with a Roman Catholic or Church of England parish? YES   NO   ☐ 38

7. Additional Features

(a) At present is your school roll:

falling?	1
static?	2
rising?	3

☐ 39

N.B. For the purpose of this questionnaire, please record a static roll, unless changes in either direction have exceeded 10% in the last year, or 5% a year for the last three years.

(b) What percentage of your staff have come to the school within the last two years?

Under 10%	1
10–25%	2
26–50%	3
51–75%	4
76% or over	5

☐ 40

(c) Were you appointed to the school as head-teacher

Under 2 years ago?	1
2–5 years ago?	2
Over 5 years ago?	3

☐ 41

(d) Do you have a special unit attached to the school, e.g. for the partially hearing or the partially sighted? YES / NO

☐ 42

8. Background Information

(a) Which of the following best describes the parents of the children in your school?

Largely non-professional, unskilled working population	1
Mainly skilled or semi-skilled but non-professional working population	2
Large number of professional or managerial workers	3
A mixed community, not adequately described by 1, 2 or 3	4

☐ 43

(b) Is your locality characterized by high unemployment (over 20%)? YES / NO

☐ 44

(c) Would you please indicate the ethnic origin of the children attending your school. Please tick all the appropriate boxes.

	1. *Under 10%*	2. *10–30%*	3. *31–60%*	4. *Over 60%*	
British					☐ 45
Asian origin					☐ 46
W. Indian origin					☐ 47
Mixed origin					☐ 48
Other origin					☐ 49

(d) What percentage of your children receive free school dinners (exclude part-time children from your calculations)?

Under 10%	1
10–25%	2
26–50%	3
51–75%	4
76% and over	5

☐ 50

(e) What percentage of the mothers of your children go out to work (include full- and part-time work)?

Below 10%	1
10–25%	2
26–50%	3
51–75%	4
76% and over	5

☐ 51

(f) Excluding your normal school intake what percentage of your children (i) join, (ii) leave your school each year?

(i)			(ii)		
Under 10%	1		Under 10%	1	
10–20%	2		10–20%	2	
21–30%	3	☐ 52	21–30%	3	☐ 53
31–40%	4		31–40%	4	
41% and over	5		41% and over	5	

(g) Do any of your pupils have in-school behaviour problems which might be related to their home and family circumstances?

YES
NO   ☐ 54

If yes, roughly what percentage of your children are involved?

———————

☐ 55

Please give details of the kind of home and family circumstances
which you feel might be the cause of these in-school problems:

. . . .
. . . .
. . . .
. . . .
. . . .
. . . .
. . . .
. . . .
. . . .

56—63

9. Parental Involvement

(a) Does your school have a PTA or other formal parent
    association?   YES
                                                                        NO   64

    If no, do you have a less formal parents committee or   YES
    'Friends of the School'?   NO   65

    If your answer to either of the above questions is 'yes'
    would you please indicate below the basic aims and
    objectives of the association/committee. (Please circle
    as many numbers as are appropriate.)

    To provide a close link between home and school   1   66
    To give parents and teachers a better understanding of   2   67
    each other's problems
    To raise funds for use by the association/committee or by   3   68
    the school or both
    To inform parents of the school's teaching methods and   4   69
    educational philosophy
    To provide a point of contact between the school and the   5   70
    community in which it is situated

Aims and objectives not covered by the above (please specify)   6 ☐
                                                                      71

. . . .

. . . .

. . . .

(b) Are your new parents invited to visit the school before their   YES ☐
     children start to attend?   NO   72

(c) Are new parents sent any written information about the   YES ☐
     school before their children start to attend?   NO   73

10. Methods of Involvement

(a)   (i) Are parents invited to attend open days or open evenings? YES ☐
                                                                     NO   74

     (ii) If yes, how often do these take place?
          Once or twice a year   1
          Once a term   2   ☐
          Twice a term   3   75
          More often   4

     (iii) Roughly what percentage of your children have parents
           or guardians attending on these occasions?
           Under 20%   1
           20–50%   2   ☐
           51–75%   3   76
           76% and over   4

                                                                  ☐☐
                                                                  79 80

                                              ☐☐☐☐☐☐☐
                                                  1–7

     (iv) Please indicate whether your open days or open evenings
          take any of the following forms?
          Exhibitions of project work completed by one or two   YES ☐
          classes or the whole school   NO   8
          Displays of general work undertaken by children   YES ☐
                                                                       NO   9
          Formal discussions between parents and teacher   YES ☐
          concerning their child's work and progress   NO   10
          Parents invited into the classrooms to see their   YES ☐
          children at work   NO   11

School prize-giving day
YES
NO ☐ 12

Harvest festival and/or Christmas nativity play
YES
NO ☐ 13

Summer fete, sports day, etc.
YES
NO ☐ 14

Other (please specify)
YES
NO ☐ 15

. . . .

. . . .

(b) (i) Apart from open days, is provision made for parents to discuss their children's work or problems by appointment with the teachers or the head?
YES
NO ☐ 16

(ii) If yes, do parents come:
On a regular basis? 1 ☐ 17

When they want to discuss a particular problem? 2 ☐ 18

When specifically asked to come by the head or their child's teacher? 3 ☐ 19

Irregularly, 'just to check up on things'? 4 ☐ 20

(iii) Instead of or in addition to the above please indicate the nature of any 'informal' contact between parents and teachers or head:

Parents chat with teacher when leaving their children at school in the morning or picking them up in the afternoon
YES
NO ☐ 21

Parents drop in to see head when they feel the need arises
YES
NO ☐ 22

Parents invited to visit teachers and/or head at end of school day
YES
NO ☐ 23

Parents discuss their social or marital problems with the head, as well as those relating to their children
YES
NO ☐ 24

(iv) What percentage of your parents would you estimate have discussed their child with the head or his/her teacher either informally or by appointment within the last year?
Under 20% 1
20–50% 2
51–80% 3 ☐ 25
81% and over 4

(c)   (i) Do parents help with fund-raising activities in any way?   YES ☐
                                                                        NO ☐ 26

    (ii) If yes, would you please indicate below what form these
        activities might take. (Please circle as many numbers as
        are appropriate.)

        Jumble sales, summer fete, bazaars, good-as-new sales, etc.   1 ☐ 27

        Raffles, sponsored walks or other activities   2 ☐ 28

        Sales of Christmas cards, school photographs, etc.   3 ☐ 29

        Donations of money or goods   4 ☐ 30

        Dances or parties held more as social events than for fund   5 ☐ 31
        raising

    (iii) Are the funds raised in the above manner:
        Contributed to the School Fund?   1
        Given to charity?   2
        Used by parents themselves?   3 ☐ 32
        A mixture of these?   4

    (iv) Please indicate what percentage of your parents support
        these activities in *whatever capacity*:
        Under 20%   1
        20–50%   2
        51–80%   3 ☐ 33
        81% and over   4

(d)   (i) Are parents invited to workshop meetings at the school   YES
        to discuss the work their children do, methods of   NO ☐ 34
        assessment, etc.?

    (ii) If yes, how often do these meetings take place?
        Once or twice a year   1
        Once a term   2
        When the head feels it to be necessary   3 ☐ 35
        When parents request it   4

    (iii) Are the methods used at the school explained to new   YES
        parents at an initial meeting?   NO ☐ 36

    (iv) Are workshop meetings ever included as part of another   YES
        social event?   NO ☐ 37

(e) Please indicate on the list below any school-based activities in which parents may be involved. Please circle as many numbers as are applicable in the appropriate category(ies).

	Nursery	Infant or First	Junior or Middle	
Parents help on school visits and outings	1	2	4	☐ 38
Parents provide transport for football, etc., matches at other schools	1	2	4	☐ 39
Parents help dress children after PE or swimming	1	2	4	☐ 40
Parents help in school library, covering books, etc.	1	2	4	☐ 41
Parents help with craft work, cooking, music, etc., under supervision of teacher	1	2	4	☐ 42
Parents hear children read under supervision of teacher	1	2	4	☐ 43
Parents help generally in classroom, putting out materials, cleaning up at end of day, etc.	1	2	4	☐ 44
Parents with specialist knowledge, e.g. local policeman, fireman, etc., give talks to children	1	2	4	☐ 45
Parents do sewing (e.g. costumes for Christmas play) and minor repairs to school equipment	1	2	4	☐ 46
Parents do major repairs and/or alterations to school building (e.g. turn cloakrooms into classrooms)	1	2	4	☐ 47
Parents help with football, after-school clubs, etc.	1	2	4	☐ 48
Parents run or help with a holiday play scheme	1	2	4	☐ 49
Parents run a library scheme for the school	1	2	4	☐ 50
Parents help in other ways. Please given details	1	2	4	☐ 51

(f) Please indicate to what extent you have encountered any of the following problems in any attempt you may have made to involve parents.

Please record your answers as follows:

1 significant problem
2 minor problem
3 no real problem

Lack of confidentiality on the part of some parents; e.g. parents gossiping between each other about some children's inability to read, their bad behaviour, etc. 1 . 2 . 3 □ 52

Presence of parents in classroom causes behaviour problems in children 1 . 2 . 3 □ 53

Complaints from those parents not involved about those who are 1 . 2 . 3 □ 54

Staff unwilling to allow parents into their classrooms 1 . 2 . 3 □ 55

Parents unreliable in the time and amount they turn up to help 1 . 2 . 3 □ 56

Parents too eager, try to take over class from teachers or school from head 1 . 2 . 3 □ 57

Parents more interested in their own child than the class as a whole 1 . 2 . 3 □ 58

Parents do not fully understanding the aims of the school, so tend to criticize what teachers do 1 . 2 . 3 □ 59

Parents wish to help in the school for the wrong reasons, e.g. because they are bored at home 1 . 2 . 3 □ 60

Parents apathetic, unwilling to take the least interest in the school and its activities 1 . 2 . 3 □ 61

Many of the mothers working so they cannot come into the school to help 1 . 2 . 3 □ 62

Problems in attracting parents who either can't or don't want to visit the school 1 . 2 . 3 □ 63

Problems of involving parents who have difficulty in speaking English 1 . 2 . 3 □ 64

Other — please specify 1 . 2 . 3 □ 65

□□
79 80

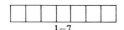

1−7

11. General Aspects

(a) Does the school provide any after-school care facilities for children, either with or without the help of parents? YES / NO □ 8

(b) Does the school run any after-school clubs, or activities which serve the general purpose of (A)? YES / NO □ 9

(c) Does the school have any room, hut, etc., set aside for use by parents or other members of the community? YES / NO □ 10

(d) Are any facilities open for the use of the community after school hours? YES / NO □ 11

(e) (i) Does the school publish a newsletter to inform parents of general school activities? YES / NO □ 12

(ii) If yes, is it produced?
Once or twice a year? 1
Once or twice a term? 2
Once a month? 3 □ 13
More often? 4

(f) (i) Are written reports concerning children's work and/or behaviour sent to parents? YES / NO □ 14

(ii) If yes, are they sent:
Once a year? 1
Twice a year? 2
Once a term? 3 □ 15
More often? 4

(g) (i) What percentage of the teaching staff live in the same locality as the pupils?
Under 10% 1
10–30% 2
31–50% 3 □ 16
51–70% 4
71% and over 5

(ii) What percentage of non-teaching staff live in the same locality as the pupils?
Under 10% 1
10–30% 2
31–50% 3 □ 17
51–70% 4
71% and over 5

(h) (i) Are any of your children 'bussed' to school from areas   YES
         outside the school's immediate locality?   NO   ☐ 18

     (ii) If yes, what percentage of your children do they
          represent?
          Under 15%   1
          15–30%   2
          31–50%   3   ☐ 19
          51% and over   4

(i) (i) Do you, as head-teacher, or do any of the teaching staff   YES
         make home visits as a matter of school policy?   NO   ☐ 20

     (ii) Alternatively, is home visiting carried out as a matter   YES
          of school policy by some other person attached to the   NO   ☐ 21
          school; e.g. home-liaison officer, social worker, health
          visitor or parish priest?

(j) (i) Does your school have a Board of Managers/Governors?   YES
                                                                               NO   ☐ 22

     (ii) If yes, are parents elected or coopted on to this Board?   YES
                                                                               NO   ☐ 23

     (iii) What percentage of the Board do they represent?
           10–20%   1
           21–50%   2   ☐ 24
           51% or over   3

(k) Are parents consulted about the inclusion of sex education   YES
     in the school curriculum and/or the showing of such films   NO   ☐ 25
     as 'Never Talk to Strangers'?

(l) Do parents play any other part in decisions concerning the   YES
     content and/or organization of the curriculum?   NO   ☐ 26
     If yes, would you please give brief details.

     . . . .

     . . . .

     . . . .

12. Aims and Attitudes

(a) As a general principle, would you like to see:
     (i) a greater number of parents involved in school activities? YES
                                                                       NO   ☐ 27

      (ii) parents involved in a wider variety of school activities than at present?   YES NO ☐ 28

or

      (iii) is there already so much parental involvement that it would not be practical to extend this further?   YES NO ☐ 29

(b) Do you have a higher level of parental involvement now than you had two years ago?   YES NO ☐ 30

(c) (i) Have your parents' attitudes to the school shown any marked change as a result of any involvement they may have had with it?   YES NO ☐ 31

    (ii) If yes, please indicate whether in your opinion their change in attitudes has taken any of the following forms:

Parents and teachers understand each other more easily   YES NO ☐ 32

Parents have a greater appreciation of the school's educational objectives   YES NO ☐ 33

Parents have a greater appreciation of the difficulties with which teachers have to contend   YES NO ☐ 34

Parents give greater support to school functions, open days, etc.   YES NO ☐ 35

Parents take a greater interest in their children's education   YES NO ☐ 36

Parents have a deeper understanding of modern educational methods in use in their children's school   YES NO ☐ 37

Parents find it easier to visit the school to talk to teachers or head   YES NO ☐ 38

Parents derive personal benefit from their involvement with school activities   YES NO ☐ 39

☐☐
79 80

(d) Irrespective of whether or not you involve parents in any school activities, we would be pleased if you would list what you consider to be the principal roles of parents in education.

. . . .

. . . .

. . . .

. . . .

. . . .

(e) Finally, we would be grateful for any further details you would
     care to give concerning the involvement of parents in your school.

     . . . .

     . . . .

     . . . .

     . . . .

     . . . .

     . . . .

     . . . .

Appendix (ii) Aspects of Parental Involvement (Questions 9 to 12 inclusive) Analysed by School Type

Notes

(i) All tables are referenced to the questionnaire (Appendix i) by the question and coding number (e.g. 9a : 64, etc.).

(ii) All percentages are reported rounded to the nearest whole number.

(iii) *Margin of error*

This survey of parental involvement in a sample of primary schools (drawn at random) was carried out in order to be able to report its extent and variety in *all* primary schools in England and Wales. To do this, the assumption is made that the way head-teachers in the sample answer each question reflects the way that heads in all schools would answer.

Clearly this is not exactly so, and when they are extrapolated to *all* primary schools, a certain margin of error exists in respect of all the percentages reported. It is, however, possible to estimate this margin of error, and to keep it always in mind when considering the information reported.

(iv) In these tables, the percentages of heads who reply 'Yes' to each question is reported for a weighted combination of primary schools (see Notes (vi) and (vii)). Where the differences between types (i.e. nursery, infant, etc.) are sufficient to be statistically significant, the percentage of each type saying 'Yes' is also reported.

(v) The following table gives the margin of error for each type of school at different levels of percentage saying 'Yes' to any question.

Percentage 'Yes'	5	10	20	30	40	50	60	70	80	90	95	
Type of school												
1. Nursery school	4	6	8	9	10	10	10	9	8	6	4	
2. Infant school with nursery class	3	4	5	6	7	7	7	6	5	4	3	
3. Infant school (no nursery class)	2	7	4	5	5	5	5	5	4	7	2	
4. JMI with nursery class	4	5	7	8	9	9	9	8	7	5	4	
5. JMI (no nursery class)	2	3	4	5	5	5	5	5	4	3	2	Percentage margins of error, *plus and minus*
6. Junior or middle-deemed-primary	2	3	5	5	6	6	6	5	5	3	2	
W.P. Weighted combination of primary schools	1	1	2	2	2	3 ▲	2	2	2	1	1	

worst cases

It can be seen that the worst case is always when 50 per cent say 'Yes' (and 50 per cent 'No'), and that the margins of error become smaller ('better') progressively as the proportions became more unequal.

An example is given, from the table in this appendix, to illustrate the way in which the margin of error should be kept in mind throughout:

Q9a:64. Does your school have a PTA or other formal parent association?

School type

1 % Yes	2 % Yes	3 % Yes	4 % Yes	5 % Yes	6 % Yes	W.P. % Yes	Sig.
7	21	29	36	40	39	35	0.001

(W.P. is the combination of all other types)

For the primary schools combined, the margin of error for the 35 per cent 'Yes' response is plus or minus two per cent. The 'true' proportion of all primary schools in England and Wales having a PTA is probably somewhere between 33 and 37 per cent.

For infant schools with no nursery class (Type 3) the margin of error for 29 per cent 'Yes' response is plus or minus five per cent. The 'true' proportion of such schools with a PTA is thus somewhere between 24 and 34 per cent.

From these examples it can be seen that the percentage reported in the tables is always the middle point of a range. This, and the size of the range should always be kept in mind.

(vi) *The need for weighting*

The critical decision which has to be made at the beginning of a project of this kind is how large a sample can be afforded, and what margins of error are thus implied. To maintain the agreed margins of error for the least numerous types of primary school (nursery) would require the drawing of a very much larger sample overall, if it were simply drawn randomly from primary schools as a whole.

It was intended that a five per cent margin of error would be maintained for all types, except nursery where it would be 10 per cent *at the worst* level (i.e. 50 per cent saying 'Yes'). The subsequent decision to 'split' one sample, and low returns of questionnaires from junior schools undermined this to a certain extent.

The obvious way of economizing when there is an interest in schools as primary schools and, at a more precise level, as particular *types* of primary school, is to draw random samples of each type, sufficiently large to maintain acceptable margins of error.

(vii) However, adopting this economical option results in the total sample not being correctly proportioned by type, and before the data from each type can be combined, it is necessary first to 'weight' it. The number of schools *do not*, as a direct consequence, 'add up' in any simple manner. To avoid the confusion which this might cause, percentages only (and not actual numbers) are reported in the tables in Appendix (ii) and (iv), and in the chapters which refer to them.

(viii) The actual sample sizes *achieved* (i.e. the number of question-naires returned) were as follows:

Types of schools	*Number*
1. Nursery school	93
2. Infant school with nursery class	213
3. Infant school (no nursery class)	344
4. JMI with nursery class	126
5. JMI (no nursery class)	332
6. Junior or middle-deemed-primary	293
Total (unweighted)	1,401

Technically it is more accurate to call the 'margins of error' the 'Confidence Limit'. It is calculated from the standard deviation of a percentage which is given by

$$100 \times \sqrt{pq/n}$$

where p = the proportion of sample positive responses,
       q = the proportion of sample negative responses,
       n = the number in the sample.

The confidence with which limits may be expressed is determined by the distribution of proportions. Thus if one wishes to be 95 per cent confident that the 'true' score falls within the limits set, the term becomes

$$100 \times 1.96\sqrt{pq/n}.$$

Question		1	2	3	4	5	6	WP	Sig.
		%	%	%	%	%	%	%	
9a:64		7	21	29	36	40	39	35	<0.001
9a:65								26	NS
9a:66								56	NS
9a:67								51	NS
9a:68								55	NS
9a:69								42	NS
9a:70								39	NS
9a:71								9	NS
9b:72		99	98	97	95	96	74	92	<0.001
9c:73		41	62	73	56	64	67	66	<0.001
10a:74		74	99	98	95	98	99	97	<0.001
10a:75	1	23	43	44	52	59	54	52	
	2	40	33	35	32	25	34	30	<0.001
	3	12	10	10	6	6	6	7	
	4	2	10	9	6	7	5	7	
10a:76	1	6	2	1	3	1	1	1	
	2	15	11	7	17	10	11	10	<0.001
	3	26	31	17	36	24	31	24	
	4	29	53	72	40	63	54	61	
10a:08		14	47	54	56	51	62	53	<0.001
10a:09		49	84	86	83	83	87	84	<0.001
10a:10		14	83	89	90	87	92	87	<0.001
10a:11		54	59	48	57	36	43	43	<0.001
10a:12		1	1	3	20	14	9	10	<0.001
10a:13		49	92	95	90	94	89	92	<0.001
10a:14		44	71	78	89	91	90	85	<0.001
10a:15								36	NS
10b:16		80	94	98	98	98	99	98	<0.001
10b:17								9	NS
10b:18		69	91	95	94	96	97	95	<0.001
10b:19		32	72	69	67	64	76	67	<0.001
10b:20								31	NS
10b:21		99	99	95	97	96	68	91	<0.001
10b:22								96	NS
10b:23		37	60	60	59	58	46	56	<0.001
10b:24		93	91	86	82	73	85	80	<0.001
10b:25	1	1	8	7	14	11	13	10	
	2	11	25	17	25	19	25	19	<0.001
	3	30	35	22	35	27	25	26	
	4	58	32	54	26	42	36	43	
10c:26								96	NS
10c:27								87	NS
10c:28		69	71	63	86	71	78	69	<0.001
10c:29								75	NS
10c:30								58	NS
10c:31		38	30	38	41	48	46	42	<0.001
10c:32	1	67	41	35	39	32	30	33	
	2	0	0	1	0	1	1	1	<0.001
	3	0	0	0	1	2	3	1	
	4	33	59	64	61	64	66	61	

Question		1	2	3	4	5	6	WP	Sig.
		%	%	%	%	%	%	%	
10c:33	1	2	2	2	6	1	5	2	
	2	11	17	11	20	13	20	14	<0.001
	3	29	42	35	45	41	46	39	
	4	58	38	52	28	45	29	41	
10d:34								34	NS
10d:35	1	5	11	10	13	11	13	11	
	2	2	4	3	3	2	3	2	<0.001
	3	6	20	22	15	17	19	18	
	4	6	3	3	3	4	3	3	
10d:36		57	61	76	56	58	58	63	<0.001
10d:37								14	NS
10e:38								78	NS
10e:39		3	9	17	62	74	80	54	<0.001
10e:40		13	27	29	22	20	9	20	<0.001
10e:41		26	33	37	20	24	29	29	<0.001
10e:42		32	48	48	30	33	26	36	<0.001
10e:43								26	NS
10e:44		33	36	28	25	15	8	19	<0.001
10e:45								45	NS
10e:46								65	NS
10e:47								10	NS
10e:48		2	7	9	34	29	32	22	<0.001
10e:49								7	NS
10e:50								4	NS
10e:51								19	NS
		S M	S M	S M	S M	S M	S M	S M	
*10f:52								7 25	NS
10f:53		12 31	5 21	4 16	2 18	4 14	2 6	4 14	<0.001
10f:54								3 10	NS
10f:55								8 15	NS
10f:56								5 13	NS
10f:57								3 4	NS
10f:58								7 19	NS
10f:59								3 15	NS
10f:60								3 11	NS
10f:61		7 24	7 24	4 19	15 29	9 20	13 25	8 21	<0.001
10f:62		10 26	33 31	25 34	23 33	21 27	34 22	25 28	<0.001
10f:63								18 28	NS
10f:64		17 13	12 14	6 12	15 12	5 4	7 7	7 8	<0.001
*10f:65								3 2	NS
11a:08		4	10	7	20	14	14	12	<0.001
11b:09		2	11	10	52	39	60	33	<0.001
11c:10		15	11	12	21	6	10	9	<0.001
11d:11		5	24	30	44	40	47	37	<0.001
11e:12		24	44	55	59	61	63	58	<0.001
11e:13	1	5	7	9	9	8	11	9	
	2	13	22	26	35	34	36	31	<0.001
	3	3	4	7	7	8	6	7	
	4	1	9	13	9	12	10	11	

Question		1	2	3	4	5	6	WP	Sig.
School Type is the span over columns 1–6 and WP									

Question		1	2	3	4	5	6	WP	Sig.
		%	%	%	%	%	%	%	
11f:14		1	8	18	63	62	77	49	<0.001
11f:15	1	0	6	15	48	51	57	39 ⎫	
	2	0	0	0	14	7	16	7 ⎪	<0.001
	3	0	0	0	2	1	2	1 ⎬	
	4	1	1	1	0	1	1	1 ⎭	
11f:16	1	64	63	52	67	45	51	50 ⎫	
	2	6	11	17	15	20	27	20 ⎪	
	3	11	15	15	12	16	10	14 ⎬	<0.001
	4	9	4	6	4	10	4	7 ⎪	
	5	6	5	9	3	9	5	8 ⎭	
11g:17	1	52	51	33	34	17	26	26 ⎫	
	2	8	7	5	12	6	7	6 ⎪	
	3	13	10	10	9	8	6	8 ⎬	<0.001
	4	6	7	7	9	9	11	8 ⎪	
	5	16	23	44	32	59	47	49 ⎭	
11h:18		24	18	24	33	41	25	31	<0.001
11h:19	1	14	11	15	21	18	18	17 ⎫	
	2	5	2	6	6	10	4	7 ⎪	<0.001
	3	2	1	2	2	6	2	4 ⎬	
	4	3	2	1	6	7	2	4 ⎭	
11i:20		34	25	12	34	21	23	20	<0.001
11i:21								48	NS
11j:22		87	91	96	94	98	94	96	<0.001
11j:23								67	NS
11j:24								54 ⎫	
								12 ⎬	NS
								1 ⎭	
11k:25		4	26	29	52	48	61	43	<0.001
11l:26								4	NS
12a:27		53	66	54	72	57	67	59	<0.001
12a:28								52	NS
12a:29		28	15	26	9	20	14	20	<0.001
12b:30								55	NS
12c:31								63	NS
12c:32								59	NS
12c:33								54	NS
12c:34								58	NS
12c:35								47	NS
12c:36								48	NS
12c:37								38	NS
12c:38								61	NS
12c:39		62	67	57	50	44	50	50	<0.001

---

*For questions 10f:52–10f:65 inclusive, responses are subdivided into severe (S) and minor (M).

Appendix (iii) Typology of Parental Involvement

Table 1: Questions characteristic of parental involvement

Q9a:64, Q9a:65, Q9b:72, Q9c:73, Q10a:74, Q10b:16, Q10b:21, Q10b:22, Q10b:23, Q10b:24, Q10c:26, Q10d:34, Q10d:36, Q10e, Q10e:38, Q103:39, Q10e:40, Q10e:41, Q103:42, Q10e:43, Q10e:44, Q10e:45, Q10e:46, Q10e:47, Q10e:48, Q10e:49, Q10e:50, Q10e:51, Q10f, Q10f:52, Q10f:53, Q10f:54, Q10f:55, Q10f:56, Q10f:57, Q10f:58, Q10f:59, Q10f:60, Q10f:61, Q10f:62, Q10f:63, Q10f:64, Q10f:65, Q11a:8, Q11b:9, Q11c:10, Q11d:11, Q11e:12, Q11f:14, Q11h:18, Q11i:20, Q11i:21, Q11j:23, Q11l:26.

Table 2: Characteristics of parental involvement in rank order of discrimination between infant and nursery schools (younger) and all other primary schools (older)

Rank		Direction	Rank		Direction
1	Q10e:39	Older	17	Q10f:53	Younger
2	Q11f:14	Older	18	Q10f:55	Older
3	Q10e:38	Older	19	Q10f:60	Older
4	Q11b:9	Older	20	Q11j:23	Younger
5	Q10f:61	Older	21	Q10e:48	Older
6	Q10b:21	Younger	22	Q10c:26	Younger
7	Q10e:46	Older	23	Q11h:18	Older
8	Q10d:36	Younger	24	Q11j:22	Older
9	Q10e:45	Older	25	Q10f:62	Older
10	Q10b:24	Younger	26	Q10b:16	Older
11	Q10e:40	Older	27	Q11e:26	Older
12	Q9c:73	Younger	28	Q10e:50	Older
13	Q10e:44	Younger	29	Q10f:56	Older
14	Q10e:43	Older	30	Q10e:51	Older
15	Q9b:72	Younger	31	Q10f:57	Older
16	Q10f:59	Older	32	Q10d:34	Older

Table 2 — *continued*

Rank		Direction	Rank		Direction
33	Q10b:22	Younger	43	Q10a:74	Older
34	Q9a:65	Younger	44	Q10e:41	Older
35	Q10e:47	Older	45	Q10f:52	Older
36	Q9a:64	Older	46	Q11a:8	Older
37	Q10h:23	Younger	47	Q11e:12	Older
38	Q11i:20	Older	48	Q11c:10	Younger
39	Q10f:58	Older	49	Q10f:64	Younger
40	Q10e:42	Older	50	Q11d:11	Older
41	Q10f:65	Older	51	Q11i:21	Younger
42	Q10f:63	Older			

Table 3: Rank order of discriminators for each group

(a) Younger

Rank

1	Q10b:21	Parents chat with teacher when collecting and bringing children, casually, daily.
2	Q10d:36	Methods of school explained to parents at initial meeting.
3	Q10b:24	Parents discuss social or marital problems with head.
4	Q9c:73	New parents sent written information about school before children start to attend.
5	Q10e:44	Parents help generally in classroom.
6	Q9b:72	New parents invited to visit school before children start to attend.
7	Q10f:53	Presence of parents in classroom causes behaviour problems in children.
8	Q11j:23	Parents coopted on to managing body.
9	Q10c:26	Parents help with fund raising.
10	Q10b:22	Parents drop in to see head when they feel the need arises.
11	Q9a:65	'Less formal' parents committee.
12	Q10b:23	Parents invited to visit teachers and/or head at the end of the school day.
13	Q11c:10	School has room, hut, etc., set aside for parents or members of community.
14	Q10f:64	Problems of involving parents who have difficulty speaking English.
15	Q11i:21	Home visiting as a matter of school policy by 'other person'.

Table 3 – *continued*

Rank

(b) Older

1	Q10e:39	Parents provide transport for football, etc., matches at other schools.
2	Q11f:14	Written reports concerning children's work and/or behaviour sent to parents.
3	Q10e:38	Parents help on school visits and outings.
4	Q11b:9	School runs after-school clubs or activities which serve general purpose of after-school care (11B:8).
5	Q10f:61	Parents apathetic, unwilling to take the least interest in school and its activities.
6	Q10e:46	Parents do sewing (e.g. costumes for Christmas play) and minor repairs to school equipment.
7	Q10e:45	Parents with specialist knowledge (e.g. local policeman, fireman, etc.) give talks to children.
8	Q10e:40	Parents help dress children after PE or swimming.
9	Q10e:43	Parents hear children read under supervision of teacher.
10	Q10f:59	Parents do not fully understand the aims of the school, so tend to criticize what teachers do.
11	Q10f:55	Staff unwilling to allow parents into their classrooms.
12	Q10f:60	Parents wish to help in the school for the wrong reasons, e.g. because they are bored at home.
13	Q10e:48	Parents help with football, after-school clubs, etc.
14	Q11h:18	Children 'bussed' to school from areas outside school's immediate locality.
15	Q11j:22	School has Board of Managers.
16	Q10f:62	Many mothers working so that they cannot come into school and help.
17	Q10b:16	Provision made for parents to discuss children's work or problems by appointment with teachers or head.
18	Q11e:26	Parents play part in decisions concerning the content and organization of curriculum.
19	Q10e:50	Parents run library scheme for school.
20	Q10f:56	Parents unreliable in the time and amount they turn up to help.
21	Q10e:51	Parents help in various ways (open-ended).
22	Q10f:57	Parents too eager, try to take over the class from teacher, or school from the head.
23	Q10d:34	Parents invited to workshop meetings at the school to discuss the work children do, and methods of assessment.

Table 3 – *continued*

Rank

24	Q10e:47	Parents do major repairs and for alterations to school building (e.g. turn cloakrooms into class-rooms).
25	Q9a:64	School has PTA or other formal parent association.
26	Q11i:20	Head-teacher or teaching staff visit homes as a matter of school policy.
27	Q10f:58	Parents more interested in own child than the class as a whole.
28	Q10e:42	Parents help with craft work.
29	Q10f:65	Various problems (open-ended).
30	Q10f:63	Problems of attracting parents who can't or don't want to visit the school.
31	Q10a:74	Parents invited to attend open days or evenings.
32	Q10e:41	Parents help in school library, covering books, etc.
33	Q10f:52	Lack of confidentiality on the part of parents.
34	Q11a:8	School provides after-school *care* facilities for children.
35	Q11e:12	School publishes newletter.
36	Q11d:11	Facilities open for the use of community after school hours.

Appendix (iv) Factors Influencing Parental Involvement

N.B. (i) All percentages rounded to the nearest whole number.
(ii) Tables 1–23 inclusive report data on a weighted combination[1] of all types of primary schools.

---

[1] See Appendix (ii), Note (vi).

Table 1: Association between school location and type of parental employment

	School Location								All Types
	1	*2*	*3*	*4*	*5*	*6*	*7*	*8*	
Type of Employment	% of schools	% of schools	% of schools	% of schools	% of schools	% of schools	% of schools	% of schools	% of schools
Largely non-professional, unskilled working population	81	76	67	22	0	0	12	12	24
Mainly skilled or semi-skilled but non-professional working population	13	20	25	39	20	10	16	10	22
Large number of professional or managerial workers	0	4	0	1	41	64	7	12	10
A mixed community not adequately described by the above	6	0	8	38	39	26	65	66	44

Chi-squared
p = <0.001   Cramer's V = 0.38†

Key to School Location
1. Houses are closely packed together with many in a poor state of repair.
2. An area of council housing characterized by high-rise flats.
3. An area dominated by a large council estate.
4. An area of mixed council and privately owned housing of the less expensive type.
5. An urban/suburban area of mostly private housing.
6. A suburban private housing estate with large houses.
7. A rural or semi-rural area.
8. An area of mixed housing covering two or more categories.

† Cramer's V statistic provides an index of the degree of relationship between the cross-tabulated categories. Cramer's V may take values from 0 (complete independence) to 1 (complete interdependence).

Table 2: Association between school location and the percentage of children receiving free school meals

	School Location								All Areas
% of Children Receiving Free School Meals	*1* % of schools	*2* % of schools	*3* % of schools	*4* % of schools	*5* % of schools	*6* % of schools	*7* % of schools	*8* % of schools	% of schools
Under 10%	8	4	8	45	91	100	76	58	53
10–25%	42	36	49	45	8	0	18	33	32
26% and over	50	60	43	10	1	0	6	9	15

Chi-squared
p = <0.001   Cramer's **V** = 0.28

Key to School Location
1. Houses are closely packed together with many in a poor state of repair and with some multi-occupation.
2. An area of council housing characterized by high-rise flats.
3. An area dominated by a large council estate.
4. An area of mixed council and privately owned housing of the less expensive type.
5. An urban/suburban area of mostly private housing.
6. A suburban private housing estate with large, detached or semi-detached houses.
7. A rural or semi-rural area.
8. An area of mixed housing covering two or more of the above categories.

Table 3: Association between type of parental employment and the percentage of children receiving free school meals

	Type of Employment				
	1	*2*	*3*	*4*	*All*
% of Children Receiving Free School Meals	*% of schools*	*% of schools*	*% of schools*	*% of schools*	*% of schools*
Under 10%	14	49	94	69	54
10–25%	44	44	6	25	32
26% and over	42	7	0	6	14

Chi-squared
p = <0.001   Cramer's V = 0.31.

Key for Type of Employment
1. Largely non-professional, unskilled working population.
2. Mainly skilled or semi-skilled but non-professional working population.
3. Large number of professional or managerial workers.
4. A mixed community, not adequately described by the above.

Table 4: Association between type of parental involvement and school location

Type of Parental Involvement	School Location								All areas	Cramer's V
	1	2	3	4	5	6	7	8		
	% of schools	% of schools	% of schools	% of schools	% of schools	% of schools	% of schools	% of schools	% of schools	
Parents provide transport for football, etc., matches at other schools	33	46	39	48	59	74	71	55	54	0.23
Parents help dress children after PE or swimming	12	8	15	16	30	29	22	25	20	0.13
Parents help in school library, covering books, etc.	22	23	28	32	40	50	17	32	29	0.17
Parents help with craft work, cooking, music, etc., under supervision of teacher	30	19	31	38	55	53	27	40	36	0.17
Parents help generally in classroom, putting out materials, cleaning up at end of day, etc.	16	19	20	20	35	13	9	22	19	0.18
Parents with specialist knowledge, e.g. local policeman, fireman, etc., give talks to children	25	38	35	46	62	55	51	39	45	0.17
Parents help with football, after-school clubs, etc.	22	8	16	20	32	47	21	24	22	0.14
All schools	4	2	12	26	8	3	21	24	100	

Chi-squared p = <0.001 in all cases

Key to School Location:
1. Houses are closely packed together in a poor state of repair.
2. An area of council housing characterized by high-rise flats.
3. An area dominated by a large council estate.
4. An area of mixed council and privately owned housing of the less expensive type.
5. An urban/suburban area of mostly private houses.
6. A suburban private housing estate with large houses.
7. A rural or semi-rural area.
8. An area of mixed housing covering two or more categories.

Table 5: Association between type of parental involvement and the percentage of children receiving free school meals

	% of Children Receiving Free School Meals				
	Under 10%	*10–25%*	*26% and over*		
Type of Parental Involvement	*% of schools*	*% of schools*	*% of schools*	*Totals*	*Cramer's V*
Parents provide transport for football, etc., matches at other schools	62	48	39	54	0.18
Parents help dress children after PE or swimming	25	14	17	20	0.12
Parents help with craft work, cooking, etc., under supervision of teacher	41	31	29	36	0.11
Parents with specialist knowledge, e.g. local policeman, fireman, etc., give talks to children	50	40	35	45	0.12
All schools	53	33	14	100	

Chi-squared $p = <0.001$ in all cases

Table 6: Association between type of parental involvement and type of parental employment

Type of Parental Involvement	|Type of employment					
	1	*2*	*3*	*4*	*All types*	
	% of schools	% of schools	% of schools	% of schools	% of schools	Cramer's V
Parents help on school visits and outings	74	73	89	81	78	0.11
Parents provide transport for football, etc., matches at other schools	37	50	68	62	54	0.22
Parents help dress children after PE or swimming	12	16	36	24	21	0.17
Parents help in school library, covering books, etc.	26	28	48	27	29	0.14
Parents help with craft work, cooking, music, etc., under supervision of teacher	29	36	52	38	37	0.13
Parents hear children read under supervision of teacher	25	20	40	27	26	0.12
Parents help generally in classroom, putting out materials, cleaning up at end of day, etc.	21	16	32	17	19	0.12
Parents with specialist knowledge, e.g. local policeman, fireman, etc., give talks to children	37	37	64	48	45	0.17
Parents do sewing (e.g. costumes for Christmas play) and minor repairs to school equipment	57	64	72	70	66	0.11
Parents help with football, after-school clubs, etc.	16	22	34	24	22	0.11
All schools	24	22	10	44	100	

Chi-squared p = <0.001 in all cases

Key to Type of Employment
1. Largely non-professional, unskilled working population.
2. Mainly skilled or semi-skilled but non-professional working population.
3. Large number of professional or managerial workers.
4. A mixed community, not adequately described by the above.

Table 7a: Association between type of parental involvement and ethnic origin of pupils: British

	Percentage British Origin				
Type of Involvement	*% of schools 1*	*% of schools 2*	*% of schools 3*	*% of schools 4*	*Cramer's V*
Parents provide transport for football, etc., matches at other schools	11	23	41	55	0.11
All schools	1	1	3	95	

Chi-squared p = <0.001

1. Under 10%
2. 10–30%
3. 31–60%   } British origin
4. Over 60%

Table 7b: Asian

	Percentage Asian Origin			
Type of Involvement	*% of schools 1*	*% of schools 2*	*% of schools 3*	*Cramer's V*
Parents provide transport for football, etc., matches at other schools	56	30	15	0.16
Parents help dress children after PE or swimming	21	8	6	0.09
All schools	93	5	2	

Chi squared p = <0.001

Table 7c: West Indian

	Percentage West Indian Origin			
Type of Involvement	% of schools 1	% of schools 2	% of schools 3	Cramer's V
Parents provide transport for football, etc., matches at other schools	55	37	20	0.10
All schools	95	4	1	

Chi-squared p = <0.001

1, Under 10% ⎤
2. 10–30%   ⎬ Asian (b) ⎤
3. Over 31% ⎦ West Indian (c) ⎬ origin

Table 8: Association between type of parental involvement and percentage of mothers who work

	Percentage of working mothers					
Type of Involvement	% of schools 1	% of schools 2	% of schools 3	% of schools 4	% of schools 5	Cramer's V
Parents hear children read under supervision of teacher	9	22	25	30	34	0.11
All schools	3	13	44	32	7	

Chi-squared p = <0.001

1. Less than 10% ⎤
2. 10–25%   ⎥
3. 26–50%   ⎬ working mothers
4. 51–75%   ⎥
5. Over 76% ⎦

Table 9: Association between type of parental involvement and annual pupil turnover

| | Pupil Turnover | | | | | |
Type of Involvement	% of schools 1	% of schools 2	% of schools 3	% of schools 4	% of schools 5	Cramer's V
Parents help on school visits and outings	76	85	86	81	86	0.10
Parents provide transport for football, etc., matches at other schools	57	52	40	15	5	0.15
Parents help with craft cooking, music, etc., under supervision of teacher	33	46	45	55	38	0.09
Parents hear children read under supervision of teacher	23	35	28	47	13	0.12
All schools	75	19	3	2	1	

Chi-squared p = <0.001 in all cases

1. Under 10%
2. 10–20%
3. 21–30% } annual pupil turnover
4. 31–40%
5. Over 41%

Table 10: Association between type of parental involvement and change in school roll

| | School Roll | | | |
| | Falling | Static | Rising | |
Type of Involvement	*% of schools*	*% of schools*	*% of schools*	*Cramer's V*
Parents with specialist knowledge, e.g. local policeman, fireman, etc., give talks to children	41	42	61	0.14
All schools	28	57	15	

Chi-squared p = <0.001.

Table 11: Association between type of parental involvement and connection with a Roman Catholic or Church of England parish

Type of Involvement	*% of schools connected*	*% of schools not con- nected*	*Phi*
Parents help with craft work, cooking, music, etc., under supervision of teacher	27	38	0.10
Parents help generally in classroom putting out materials cleaning up at end of day, etc.	12	21	0.09
Parents with specialist knowledge, e.g. local policeman, fireman, etc., give talks to children	34	47	0.10
All schools	19	81	

Chi-squared p = <0.001 in all cases

Table 12: Association between type of parental involvement and type of school architecture (infants)

Type of Parental Involvement	School Architecture					All schools	Cramer's V
	1 % of schools	2 % of schools	3 % of schools	4 % of schools	5 % of schools	% of schools	
Parents help in school library, covering books, etc.	9	25	35	29	43	27	0.21
Parents help with craft work, cooking, music, etc. under supervision of teacher	18	28	44	50	63	36	0.27
Parents hear children read under supervision of teacher	15	22	32	26	35	25	0.14
Parents help generally in classroom, putting out materials, cleaning up at end of day, etc.	9	21	25	25	35	22	0.16
Parents with specialist knowledge, e.g. local policeman, fireman, etc., talks to children	22	34	44	40	48	36	0.16
All schools	15	39	26	12	8	100	

Chi-squared p = <0.001 in all cases

Key to School Architecture
1. Traditional school. Classroom type design with no hall, or with hall separate from main school building.
2. Traditional, classroom-type design, no room available other than hall for group or communal activities.
3. As above, but some space available for integrated or small-group activities.
4. Design partially open-plan, with some classroom units.
5. Design totally open-plan, with or without partitions which may be drawn across to create classroom units.

Table 13: Association between type of parental involvement and type of curriculum organization (infants)

Type of Parental Involvement	Curriculum Organization						All schools	Cramer's V
	1 % of schools	2 % of schools	3 % of schools	4 % of schools	5 % of schools	6 % of schools	% of schools	
Parents help in school library, covering books, etc.	43	35	16	33	30	20	27	0.18
Parents help with craft work, cooking, music, etc., under supervision of teacher	68	50	21	50	39	22	36	0.28
Parents hear children read under supervision of teacher	40	33	28	31	28	17	26	0.17
Parents help generally in classroom, putting out materials, cleaning up at end of day, etc.	46	28	15	33	24	12	22	0.19
Parents do sewing (e.g. costumes for Christmas play) and minor repairs to school equipment	73	72	55	72	59	57	63	0.15
All schools	4	27	22	4	25	18	100	

Chi-squared p = <0.001 in all cases

Key to Curriculum Organization
1. Unstreamed classes, totally or partially vertically-grouped; staff organized into units for team-teaching and an integrated day approach.
2. Unstreamed classes, totally or partially vertically grouped, class rather than team-teaching with an integrated day approach.
3. As above but with traditional organization (e.g. basic subjects am and creative activities pm).
4. Unstreamed classes, horizontally grouped; team or cooperative teaching with an integrated day approach.
5. Unstreamed classes, horizontally grouped; class rather than team-teaching with an integrated day approach.
6. Unstreamed classes, horizontally grouped; generally taught by one person with a structured curriculum.

Table 14: Association between type of parental involvement and type of school architecture (junior)

| | Type of School Architecture | | | | | All schools | |
Type of Parental Involvement	1 % of schools	2 % of schools	3 % of schools	4 % of schools	5 % of schools	% of schools	Cramer's V
Parents help in school library, covering books, etc.	8	20	30	35	35	23	0.21
Parents help with craft work, cooking, music, etc. under supervision of teacher	15	19	26	51	43	26	0.27
Parents help generally in classroom, putting out materials, cleaning up at end of day, etc.	2	4	7	17	15	7	0.19
Parents help with football, after-school clubs, etc.	20	28	34	36	54	31	0.17
All schools	17	37	27	13	6	100	

Chi-squared p = <0.001 in all cases

Key to School Architecture
1. Traditional school. Classroom type design with no hall separate from main school building.
2. Traditional, classroom-type design; no room available other than hall for group or communal activities.
3. As above but some space available for integrated or small-group activities.
4. Design partially open-plan, with some classroom units.
5. Design totally open-plan with or without partitions which can be drawn across to create classroom units.

Table 15: Association between type of parental involvement and type of curriculum organization (junior)

Type of Parental Involvement	Curriculum Organization (% of Schools)							All schools	Cramer's V
	1 % of schools	2 % of schools	3 % of schools	4 % of schools	5 % of schools	6 % of schools	7 % of schools	% of schools	
Parents help with craft work, cooking, music, etc., under supervision of teacher	50	44	21	28	37	19	22	26	0.21
Parents hear children read under supervision of teacher	25	26	13	37	25	13	29	19	0.18
Parents with specialist knowledge, e.g. local policeman, fireman, etc., give talks to children	56	58	39	50	60	37	49	45	0.19
All schools	2	10	24	4	16	33	10	100	

Chi-squared p = <0.001 in all cases

Key to Curriculum Organization
1. Unstreamed classes, totally or partially vertically-grouped; staff organized into units for team-teaching and an integrated day approach.
2. Unstreamed classes, totally or partially vertically-grouped; class rather than team-teaching with an integrated day approach.
3. As above but with traditional organization (e.g. basic subjects am and creative activities pm).
4. Unstreamed classes, horizontally grouped; team- or cooperative teaching with an integrated day approach.
5. Unstreamed classes, horizontally grouped; class rather than team-teaching with an integrated day approach.
6. Unstreamed classes, horizontally grouped; generally taught by one person with a structured curriculum.
7. As above but classes streamed or setted for some or all subjects.

Table 16: Association between type of parental involvement and size of school

Type of Parental Involvement	Schools by Size (No. of Children)							Cramer's V
	50 % of schools	51–100 % of schools	101–151 % of schools	151–250 % of schools	251–350 % of schools	351 or over % of schools	All schools % of schools	
Parents provide transport for football, etc., matches at other schools	61	57	46	47	59	64	54	0.14
Parents help in school library, covering books, etc.	7	18	26	31	32	43	29	0.20
Parents help with craft work, cooking, music, etc., under supervision of teacher	22	27	33	44	39	35	36	0.14
Parents hear children read under supervision of teacher	14	20	22	29	26	36	26	0.14
Parents help generally in classroom, putting out materials, cleaning up at end of day, etc.	3	13	14	25	20	22	19	0.16
All schools	8	14	11	32	21	14	100	

Chi-squared p = <0.001 in all cases

Table 17: Association between type of parental involvement and staff—pupil ratio: infant or first

Type of Involvement	Staff—Pupil Ratio				
	% of schools 1	% of schools 2	% of schools 3	% of schools 4	Cramer's V
Parents help dress children after PE or swimming	8	19	26	26	0.12
Parents help in school library covering books, etc.	17	21	31	37	0.12
Parents help with craft work, cooking, music, etc., under supervision of teacher	21	34	41	48	0.09
Parents with specialist knowledge, e.g. local policeman, fireman, etc., give talks to children	37	35	46	52	0.10
Parents run a library scheme	1	1	5	6	0.09
All schools	7	19	64	10	

Chi-squared p = <0.001 in all cases

1. Under 15 pupils
2. 16 to 20 pupils
3. 21 to 30 pupils 　　to one member of staff†
4. 31 and over pupils

† 'A member of staff' includes teachers, welfare assistants (other than school meals assistants), NNEB trained assistants, as well as the head.

Table 18: Association between type of parental involvement and staff—pupil ratio: junior or middle

Type of Involvement	Staff—Pupil Ratio				
	% of schools 1	% of schools 2	% of schools 3	% of schools 4	Cramer's V
Parents help on school visits and outings	72	72	80	87	0.10
Parents provide transport for football, etc., matches at other schools	44	66	78	78	0.17
Parents help in school library, covering books, etc.	11	14	26	36	0.15
Parents help with craft work, cooking, music, etc., under supervision of teacher	23	16	32	40	0.10
Parents with specialist knowledge, e.g. local policeman, fireman, etc., give talks to children	29	40	47	55	0.11
Parents do sewing (e.g. costumes for Christmas play) and minor repairs to school equipment	44	56	68	69	0.12
Parents help with football, after-school clubs, etc.	1	29	30	39	0.14
All schools	4	13	67	16	

All others non-significant

Chi-squared p = <0.001 in all cases

1. Under 15 pupils ⎫
2. 16 to 20 pupils ⎪ to one member of staff†
3. 21 to 30 pupils ⎬
4. 31 and over pupils ⎭

† 'A member of staff' includes teachers, welfare assistants (other than school meals assistants), NNEB trained assistants, as well as the head.

Table 19: Association between type of parental involvement and percentage of children seen as having in-school behaviour problems attributable to home or family circumstances

Type of Parental Involvement	Percentage of Children Seen as Having In-School Behaviour Problems						
	None	Up to 5%	6–10%	11–20%	21% and over	Totals	Cramer's V
	% of schools	% of schools	% of schools	% of schools	% of schools	% of schools	
Parents provide transport for football, etc., matches at other schools	55	59	56	42	35	54	0.15
Parents help generally in classroom, putting out materials, cleaning up at end of day, etc.	13	19	18	30	30	19	0.13
Parents help with football, after-school clubs, etc.	16	24	30	18	20	22	0.13
All schools	27	36	23	8	6	100	

Chi-squared p = <0.001 in all cases

Table 20: Association between type of parental involvement and period of present head-teacher's incumbency

	Length of Incumbency			
	Under 2 years	*2–5 years*	*Over 5 years*	
Type of Involvement	*% of schools*	*% of schools*	*% of schools*	*Cramer's V*
Parents help on school visits and outings	82	84	75	0.11
Parents help in school library, covering books, etc.	34	39	23	0.16
Parents help with craft work, cooking, music, etc., under supervision of teacher	41	46	31	0.10
Parents hear children read under supervision of teacher	30	32	22	0.10
Parents help generally in classroom, putting out materials, cleaning up at end of day, etc.	20	27	15	0.12
All schools	15	26	59	

Chi-squared $p = <0.001$ in all cases

Table 21: Association between type of parental involvement and staff turnover

	Staff Turnover					
Type of Involvement	% of schools 1	% of schools 2	% of schools 3	% of schools 4	% of schools 5	Cramer's V
Parents help in school library, covering books, etc.	24	35	31	44	24	0.12
Parents help with craft work, cooking, music, etc., under supervision of teacher	32	38	43	46	49	0.07
Parents help generally in classroom, putting out materials, cleaning up at end of day, etc.	16	22	25	24	9	0.11
Parents do sewing (e.g. costumes for Christmas play) and minor repairs to school equipment	62	66	69	81	91	0.11
All schools	52	25	18	3	2	

Chi-squared $p = <0.001$ in all cases

1. Under 10%   ⎫
2. 10–25%   ⎪
3. 26–50%   ⎬ staff changes over the past two years
4. 51–75%   ⎪
5. 76% or over ⎭

Table 22: Interrelationships between factors influencing parental involvement

Statistic of association: Cramer's V (decimal point omitted). Test of significance of association: Chi-squared (categorical data) or Kendall's Tau (ordinal data) as appropriate

	Q6:37 School location	Q8:43 Parents' occupations	Q8:50 Free school meals	Q8:45 Pupils' ethnic origins	Q8:51 Working mothers	Q8:52 Pupil turnover	Q7:39 Change in school roll	Q6:38 Church connection	Q4:32 School architecture (inf)	Q4:33 School architecture (jun)	Q5:35 Curriculum org. (inf)	Q5:36 Curriculum org. (jun)	Q2:09 School size	Q2:11 Staff–pupil ratio (inf)	Q2:12 Staff–pupil ratio (jun)	Q8:54 Behaviour problems	Q7:40 Staff turnover	Q7:41 Head's incumbency
Q6:37 School location																		
Q8:43 Parents' occupations	38																	
Q8:50 Free school meals	28	31																
Q8:45 Pupils' ethnic origins	20	20	24															
Q8:51 Working mothers	13	12	14	14														
Q8:52 Pupil turnover	10	11	15	11	NS													
Q7:39 Change in school roll	19	11	08	16	09	08												
Q6:38 Church connection	13	NS	09	NS	NS	11	NS											
Q4:32 School architecture (inf)	20	11	07	NS	09	08	10	NS										
Q4:33 School architecture (jun)	24	11	09	NS	NS	09	14	14	X									
Q5:35 Curriculum org. (inf)	16	09	09	NS	11	NS	16	14	X	X								
Q5:36 Curriculum org. (jun)	17	10	NS	NS	11	09	19	16	X	X	X							
Q2:09 School size	26	16	09	NS	16	NS	18	NS	25	28	16	19						
Q2:11 Staff–pupil ratio (inf)	22	10	08	NS	11	09	10	NS	47	X	47	X	31					
Q2:12 Staff–pupil ratio (jun)	22	09	09	NS	13	09	14	NS	X	51	X	50	29	X				
Q8:54 Behaviour problems	17	16	12	20	15	07	06	09	13	13	10	14	18	12	13			
Q7:40 Staff turnover	15	09	10	09	11	06	23	NS	09	09	12	10	16	10	09	06		
Q7:41 Heads incumbency	19	12	NS	14	NS	NS	25	NS	09	09	NS	10	10	NS	NS	16	26	

p = <0.001 in all cases

Table 23: Summary of three-way contingency analyses of factors with interrelationships reaching 0.4 or more (Cramer's V)

.. p < 0.001 } Chi-squared (categorical data)
... p < 0.0001 } or Kendall's Tau (ordinal data) as appropriate

Type of Involvement	Staff–pupil ratio (infants) within school architecture	School architecture (infants) within staff–pupil ratio	Staff–pupil ratio (junior) within school architecture	School architecture (junior) within staff–pupil ratio	Staff–pupil ratio (infants) within curriculum organization	Curriculum organization (infants) within staff–pupil ratio	Staff–pupil ratio (junior) within curriculum organization	Curriculum organization (junior) within staff–pupil ratio	School architecture (infants) within curriculum organization	Curriculum organization (infants) within school architecture	School architecture (junior) within curriculum organization	Curriculum organization (junior) within school architecture
Parents:												
Q10e:38 Help on school outings	..	...										...
Q10e:39 Transport for away games	...	...		...			... ...			...		

	1	2	3	7	6	13	8	15	8
Q10e:40 Dress children after PE	⋮⋮⋮		⋮⋮			⋮⋮	⋮	⋮	
Q10e:41 Help in school library	⋮⋮	⋮⋮⋮	⋮	⋮⋮⋮	⋮⋮⋮⋮	⋮⋮	⋮⋮⋮	⋮⋮	
Q10e:42 Help with craft, music	⋮⋮	⋮⋮⋮	⋮⋮	⋮	⋮⋮	⋮	⋮⋮⋮	⋮	⋮
Q10e:43 Hear children read	⋮⋮	⋮	⋮		⋮	⋮			⋮
Q10e:44 Help generally in classroom	⋮⋮	⋮⋮	⋮		⋮	⋮⋮	⋮	⋮⋮	⋮
Q10e:45 Give 'specialist' talks	⋮				⋮⋮				⋮
Q10e:46 Do sewing and repairs		⋮	⋮						
Q10e:47 Do major repairs		⋮				⋮	⋮	⋮	
Q10e:48 Help with football		⋮				⋮	⋮	⋮	
Q10e:49 Run holiday play scheme	⋮⋮							⋮	
Q10e:50 Run library scheme			⋮	⋮				⋮	⋮
Total significance 'score'	17	11	7	7	6	8	8	15	8

References

BLYTH, W. A. L. (1965). *English Primary Education: A Sociological Description*. Vol 2: Background. London: Routledge & Kegan Paul, Chapter 2.

BRADSHAWE, J. and WEALE, J. (1978). *Free School Meals: Area Variation in Take-up*. London: Child Poverty Action Group.

BRENNAN, P. (1974). 'Glossop Centre goes all out for integration', in supplement to *Education* (22.1.74).

BROMLEY, K. C. (Ed) (1972). Investigation of the Effects of Parents Participation in Head Start. Non-technical Report. (ERIC No. ED 080216).

CAMPAIGN FOR THE ADVANCEMENT OF STATE EDUCATION (1977). *Parents' Charter*. London: CASE.

CENTRAL ADVISORY COUNCIL FOR EDUCATION (ENGLAND) (1954). *Early Leaving*. London: HMSO.

COHEN, L. (1972). 'The headteacher's point of view'. In: CRAFT, M., RAYNOR, J. and COHEN, L. (Eds) *Linking Home and School*. London: Longman. (2nd Edn).

DEPARTMENT OF EDUCATION AND SCIENCE (1968). Education Survey 5, *Parent/Teacher Relations in Primary Schools*. London: HMSO.

DEPARTMENT OF EDUCATION AND SCIENCE AND THE WELSH OFFICE (1977). *A New Partnership for Our Schools*. (Taylor Report.) London: HMSO.

DEPARTMENT OF EDUCATION AND SCIENCE. CENTRAL ADVISORY COUNCIL FOR EDUCATION (ENGLAND) (1967). *Children and Their Primary Schools*. (Plowden Report.) Vol 1. London: HMSO.

DOUGLAS, J. W. B. (1964). *The Home and the School*. London: Macgibbon and Kee.

ERAUT, M. (n.d.) Unpublished communication.

FRIED, M. (1965). 'Grieving for a lost home'. In: DUHL, L. J. (Ed) *The Urban Condition*. New York: Basic Books.

FLOUD, J. E. and HALSEY, A. H. (1957). 'Intelligence tests, social class and selection for secondary schools', *Br. J. Sociol.*, **8**, 33.

FLOUD, J. E., HALSEY, A. H. and MARTIN, F. M. (1957). *Social Class and Educational Opportunity*. London: Heinemann.

FRASER, E. D. (1959). *Home Environment and the School*. London: University of London Press. (3rd impression with postscript, 1973.)

GARVEY, A. (1977). 'Do children want parents in school?'. *Where*, No. 125.

GOODACRE, E. (1970). *School and Home*. Slough: NFER.

GREAT BRITAIN. MINISTRY OF EDUCATION (1959). *15 to 18*. A Report of the Central Advisory Council for Education. (Crowther Report.) London: HMSO.

GREAT BRITAIN. PARLIAMENT, HOUSE OF COMMONS (1977). Green Paper. *Education in Schools: A Consultative Document*. Cmnd 6869.

GREEN, L. (1968). *Parents and Teachers: Partners or Rivals?* London: Allen and Unwin.

HEDGES, G. (1972). Volunteer parental assistance in elementary schools. Unpublished PhD thesis, The Ontario Institute for Studies in Education. (ERIC Document ED 085 849).

HEGARTY, S. and LUCAS, D. (1978) *Able to Learn? – The Pursuit of Culture-Fair Assessment.* Windsor: NFER, pp. 10–11 and 70–2.

HIGHFIELD, M. E. and PINSENT, A. (1952). *A Survey of Rewards and Punishments.* London: Newnes for the NFER.

HODGES, L. (1977). 'All change', *Times Educ. Suppl.* (8.4.77), p. 6.

JENCKS, C. (1975). *Inequality.* Harmondsworth: Penguin.

LACEY, C. and BLANE, D. (1979). 'Geographic mobility and school attainment – the confounding variables', *Educ. Res.* **21**, 3, 200–6.

LYNCH, J. and PIMPLOTT, J. (1976). *Parents and Teachers.* London: Macmillan Education.

McGEENEY, P. (1969). *Parents are Welcome.* London: Longmans Green.

McINTYRE, D. (1977). 'The teacher – roles and responsibilities', *NUT Primary Education Review*, **3**, Spring.

MIDWINTER, E. (1970). *Home School Relations in Educational Priority Areas.* Liverpool EPA Occasional Papers, No. 4.

MIDWINTER, E. (1977). *Education for Sale.* London: Allen and Unwin.

NATIONAL UNION OF TEACHERS (1978). *Partnership in Education.* The NUT's Reply to the Taylor Report. London: NUT.

PEAKER, G. F. (1971). *The Plowden Children: Four Years Later.* Windsor: NFER.

PETERS, D. (1978). 'Parents into the mainstream', *Times Educ. Suppl.* (24.3.78).

SADLER, J. (1972). *Children and Road Safety: A Survey Amongst Mothers.* London: HMSO.

SHARROCK, A. (1970). *Home/School Relations.* London: Macmillan.

TAYLOR, P. H., REID, W. A., HOLLEY, B. J. and EXON, G. (1974). *Purpose, Power and Constraint in the Primary School Curriculum.* London: Macmillan.

TIZARD, B. (n.d.) Unpublished communication.

WEDGE, P. and PROSSER, H. (1973). *Born to Fail?* London: Arrow Books.

WILSON, H. and HERBERT, G. W. (1978). *Parents and Children in the Inner City.* London: Routledge and Kegan Paul.

WISEMAN, S. (1964). *Education and Environment.* Manchester: University Press.

WISEMAN, S. (1967). 'Education and environment'. In: CRAFT, M., RAYNOR, H. and COHEN, L. (Eds) *Linking Home and School.* London: Longman (2nd edn).

WOOD, A. J. (1965). Parents and the curriculum – a study of academic cooperation and its effects on children, parents and teachers. Unpublished PhD thesis, University of Southampton.

WOOD, A. and SIMPKINS, L. (1976). *Involving Parents in the Curriculum.* Billericay: A Home and School Publication.
WOODHEAD, M. (1976). *Intervening in Disadvantage.* Slough: NFER.
YOUNG, M. and McGEENEY, P. (1968). *Learning Begins at Home.* London: Routledge and Kegan Paul.

Index

PARENTAL INVOLVEMENT
IN PRIMARY SCHOOLS